Edition KWV

Die „Edition KWV" beinhaltet hochwertige Werke aus dem Bereich der Wirtschaftswissenschaften. Alle Werke in der Reihe erschienen ursprünglich im Kölner Wissenschaftsverlag, dessen Programm Springer Gabler 2018 übernommen hat.

Weitere Bände in der Reihe http://www.springer.com/series/16033

Felix Papier

Optimization of Rental Systems

Queuing Loss Theory for the Optimization of Cargo Vehicle Rental Systems

Springer Gabler

Felix Papier
Wiesbaden, Germany

Bis 2018 erschien der Titel im Kölner Wissenschaftsverlag, Köln
Dissertation Universität zu Köln, 2007

Edition KWV
ISBN 978-3-658-24312-8 ISBN 978-3-658-24313-5 (eBook)
https://doi.org/10.1007/978-3-658-24313-5

Library of Congress Control Number: 2019934952

Springer Gabler

Originally published by Kölner Wissenschaftsverlag, Köln, 2007

This Springer Gabler imprint is published by the registered company Springer Fachmedien Wiesbaden GmbH part of Springer Nature
The registered company address is: Abraham-Lincoln-Str. 46, 65189 Wiesbaden, Germany

Acknowledgements

Only after some time I found out that doing a PhD is associated with ups and downs and times without a light at the end of the corridor. What I am proud of today is less the final product than more the process that I had gone through. And with all things in life, it would not have been possible without endless help of many people, who I would like to thank.

First of all, I would like thank my supervisor Prof. Ulrich Thonemann. He led me through what is principally my complete professional life until today, from when I began working for him as a student assistant in November 2000 until now. During all the years, he always inspired me, supported me, and helped me with everything ranging from going abroad to developing professional skills. He has shaped the course of my life, for which I am honestly grateful. I also thank Prof. Ludwig Kuntz for kindly co-supervising the thesis and Prof. Carsten Homburg for heading the thesis defense.

Next, I have to mention three persons who, although not from my department, put great effort into sharing their academic and professional knowledge with me. First of all, this is Prof. Ronald Wolff from the University of California at Berkeley. Our acquaintance began with a discussion on proving convexity for loss systems which lead to a paper on that topic. He significantly enriched my research experience by introducing me to stochastic coupling, by sharing his views on referee reports, and by discussing U.S. foreign affairs. In 2006, I had the chance to visit the Hong Kong University of Science & Technology. Prof. Kaijie Zhu was so kind to invite me to Hong Kong and to introduce me to his PhD students with whom I spent six wonderful months. Dr. Eric Pfaffmann from Deutsche Bahn AG provided invaluable insight into the world of cargo logistics. Thanks to his kind supervision, I soon felt familiar in that industry.

Probably the most important thing in my time as a PhD student are the people that I met and with whom I spent time, namely Alexander Weyers, Analena Fuchs, Andreas Brinkhoff, Carolin Hüsing, Christel Fischer, Claudia Perl, Eva Wilbuer, Jan Wienpahl, Jeanette Seifert, Jingnan Zhu, Kai Hoberg, Karin Möllering, Karl-Hendrik Magnus, Kathrin Rieger, Katja Henne, Kerstin Baumgartner, Marc Albers, Marcel Sieke, Michael Becker, Nadine Holtvogt, Peer Kleinau, Raik Özsen, Sebastian Jucken, Silke Jütte, Ulf Merschmann, and Vladislav Richter. I think of all the days and nights that we spent together, working, chatting, or going out. Real friendships have emerged from these occasions.

Special thanks go to Alexander Weyers, Gerd Papier, Karin Möllering, Marcel Sieke, and Ole Nordhoff for helping me to finalize the thesis.

My family Inga, Gerd, and Gudrun have enabled me to do my PhD, cheered me up and listened to me whenever necessary (and have kept on asking when exactly I will submit the thesis). Last but not least I have to thank Julie Demichel and Skadi Jäschke for getting me back on track when I was lost and for dragging me away from the desk when I needed a break.

Cologne, September 2007 Felix Papier

Contents

List of Tables

List of Figures

List of Abbreviations

ADI	Advance demand information
ADIP	ADI policy
AI	Arbitrary arrivals and independent service times
al.	Alii
Arb.	Arbitrary
ASA	Average stationary approximation
B2B	Business to business
BMP	Benchmark policy
C.	Coils
cdf	Cumulative distribution function
cf.	Confer
Ch.	Chapter
CTMC	Continuous-Time Markov chain
DFMP	Dynamic fleet management problem
DTMC	Discrete-Time Markov chain
e.g.	Exempli gratia
EBB	Entire batch blocking
eDTMC	Embedded discrete-time Markov chain

ELM	Erlang loss model
Eq.	Equation
Ex.	Exponential
Exp.	Expected
GPS	Global positioning system
i.e.	Id est
i.i.d.	Identically and independently distributed
Ineq.	Inequality
IP	Independence properties
mio.	Million
n/a	not applicable
Par./Params.	Parameters
PASTA	Poisson arrivals see time averages
PBB	Partial batch blocking
PC	Personal computer
pdf	Probability distribution function
Poi.	Poisson
Reg.	Regulars
Rev.	Revenues
ROS	Return on sales
Sim.	Simulation
SL	Service level
SLAP	Successive linear approximation procedure
U.S.	United States
UB	Upper bound
vs.	Versus
w/o	Without
yr	Year

List of Symbols

$\mathbf{0}$	Null matrix
$\overline{\mathbf{0}}$	Null vector
$1()$	Indicator function
$\alpha()$	Auxiliary function
a	Admission decision
A	Arrival time
A	Arrival process, auxiliary matrix (Ch. 5)
β	Blocking probability
b	Discrete auxiliary variable
B	Batch size, blocking probability (Ch. 3)
B	Submatrix of Q
c	Fleet size
C	Auxiliary matrix
CL	Class indicator
δ	Row sum of a matrix
Δ	Difference
D	Diagonal matrix with eigenvalues on the diagonal
D	Departure event

$E()$	Expected value
ε	Continuous auxiliary variable
$f()$	Probability distribution function
$f^{a*}()$	a-Fold convolution of $f()$
$F()$	Cumulative distribution function
$\overline{F}()$	Complementary cumulative distribution function
Γ	Admission policy
$g()$	Probability distribution function
$G()$	Cumulative distribution function
h	Unit holding cost
i	Discrete auxiliary variable
I	Difference in system states
I_n	Identity matrix of size n
j	Discrete auxiliary variable
$J(t)$	Service completions before time t
k	Discrete auxiliary variable
$K(t)$	Service completions before time t
l_t	Leasing quantity in period t
l	Vector of leasing quantities
L	Exp. lost sales (Ch. 2), loss in profit (Chs. 4 and 5)
μ	Reciprocal of mean rental time
N	Number of busy cars
$\phi()$	PDF of standard normal distribution
$\Phi()$	CDF of standard normal distribution
π	State probability
π	State distribution

Π	Exp. profit
$\psi()$	Auxiliary function
p	Unit penalty cost
p_i	Probability of event i
$P()$	Probability
$\widetilde{P}()$	Probability generating function
$P(t)$	Transition matrix after t time units
q	Mean order size
Q	Intensity matrix
$\widetilde{\mathbf{Q}}$	Submatrix of Q
$\widehat{\mathbf{Q}}$	Submatrix of Q
λ	Arrival rate of Poisson process
r	Revenue margin
R	Set of advance demand information
σ	Standard deviation
S	System
S	Rental or service time
SL	Service level
τ	Demand leadtime
t	Time epoch
$\widehat{t}$	Time epoch
T	Number of periods (Ch. 2), threshold level (Chs. 4 and 5)
u	Auxiliary vector
$\widetilde{\mathbf{u}}$	Auxiliary vector
U	Uniformly distributed random number on $[0, 1]$
U	Matrix of eigenvectors

v	Unit leasing cost
$\mathbf{v}$	Auxiliary vector
$\widetilde{\mathbf{v}}$	Auxiliary vector
V	Served requests (Ch. 2), exp. service rate (Chs. 4 and 5)
w	Weight variable (Ch. 4), eigenvalue (Ch. 5)
x	Continuous auxiliary variable
x	Auxiliary vector
X	Departure event (Ch. 5)
X_n	Time epoch of nth service completion (Ch. 3)
Y_n	Time epoch of nth service completion
z	Continuous auxiliary variable

Chapter 1

Introduction

1.1 Motivation

The global transportation service industry grew by 4.3% in 2006. However, the cargo logistics provider industry could not translate this growth into profitability. Due to high energy and maintenance costs, the average return-on-sales of cargo logistics providers in Europe reaches just 3% (cf. DataMonitor (2003, 2005, 2007) and Ferrulli (2007)). Reducing costs by 1% would lead to an increase of return-on-sales by 32%. Thus, tight control of costs becomes a key factor for success. This is particularly important for fleet ownership costs, which typically make up a large part of total costs of cargo logistics providers.

At the same time, the cargo logistics industry experiences a phase of market concentration, such as we observe in the container shipping industry, where the market share of the 10 largest providers grew from 49% to 60% between 2000 and 2006. As a consequence, the providers and with them their vehicle fleets grow. Large rental companies accumulate hundreds of thousands of vehicles. For example, the largest European container rental company, Sea Containers Ltd., owns about 700,000 containers. The largest European rail cargo company, Railion AG, plans to invest 1,700 mio. Euros into new rail cars during the next years (cf. BRS (2006), IICL (2006), Krummheuer (2007), and Sea Containers Ltd. (2005)).

F. Papier, *Optimization of Rental Systems*, Edition KWV,
https://doi.org/10.1007/978-3-658-24313-5_1

Therefore, fleet management is becoming increasingly complex. While in the past fleet planning could be performed manually, the new vast size of the planning problem necessitates the use of advanced planning tools. These tools do currently not exist and existing research results in the field of operations research do not yet cover the new dimension of this problem.

The substantial effect of fleet planning on company profit and the size of the planning problem have inspired us to develop stochastic models of rental systems. In this thesis, we describe research that contributes to the body of known research on these systems and that can improve decision making in rental fleet planning.

In the remaining sections of this chapter, we first describe the industry of vehicle rental businesses (Section 1.2). Then, we demonstrate how we model rental businesses as stochastic models and we define a common modeling framework (Section 1.3). Finally, we describe the overall structure of the thesis and provide a short outlook into each of the following chapters (Section 1.4).

1.2 Vehicle Rental Businesses

In this section, we introduce vehicle rental businesses. Firstly, we explain the business model of rental services. We provide an answer to the questions of what a rental service is and why customers rent instead of buying vehicles. Secondly, we describe the vehicle rental industry for commercial customers by delimiting this industry from other rental industries and by analyzing the sizes of the container rental industry, the cargo rail car rental industry, and the truck rental industry, which are typical B2B vehicle rental industries.

The Business Model of Rental Services Renting a piece of equipment means that a rental company allows the customer to use its equipment for a certain period of time and the customer compensates the rental company for the service by paying a rental fee. The rental business is therefore a service industry. Services have the characteristics that they are intangible, perishable, and that their production and their consumption are not separable (cf. Van Looy et al. (2003)).

This also applies to rental services, because they are not tangible products and they have to be produced and consumed at the same time as well as in the same place. As a consequence, rental services cannot be produced to stock. The rental company is forced to maintain sufficient capacity to "produce" the rental service whenever the customer needs it. Without sufficient capacity the rental company may loose business.

The customer, on the other hand, does not own the equipment she needs but orders it from the rental company when it is needed. But why do customers of rental companies prefer to rent equipment instead of buying it? The European Rental Association (2007) states several reasons why renting equipment is useful. We describe the ones that apply best to the rental systems we consider in this thesis:

1. **Renting equipment reduces ownership costs** Fleet equipment is often better utilized if it is rented out by a rental company than if it is owned by the company which uses it. The higher utilization of rental equipment compared to other equipment leads to less ownership costs per usage, because cost of capital and depreciation are independent of the utilization.

2. **Renting equipment reduces fixed assets** If a company purchases its own equipment, the investment becomes a fixed asset and the amount of fixed assets in the balance sheet of the company increases by the purchase price. The purchase has to be financed in some way, leading to either more debt or more shareholder equity.

3. **Renting equipment provides more flexibility** Typically, B2B equipment such as cargo vehicles or machines have long life times. If a company purchases its own equipment, it has to utilize it for a long period of time before the investment becomes profitable and, therefore, the company is less flexible with its own equipment than with rented equipment if its demand for equipment changes over time.

Industry	Market Value [mio. Euro]	Fleet Size [vehicles]
Container Rental	125	800,000
Rail Car Rental	1,750	600,000
Truck Rental	2,500	100,000
Total	4,375	1,500,000

Source: DataMonitor (2006), European Commission (2007), Krummheuer (2007), UNCTAD (1999), Sea Containers Ltd. (2005), VTG AG (2007)

Table 1.1: Annual market value and fleet size in 2005 of the main B2B vehicle rental industries in Europe

4. **Renting equipment reduces risk** Safety issues and maintenance of the rental equipment typically remains the task of the rental company. Thus, the customer does not have to worry about compliance of the equipment with legal regulations or safety standards. Since in most situations, the rental company is specialized in providing a certain type of equipment, it usually has specific knowledge about current regulations.

A major disadvantage of rental equipment is availability. While someone's own equipment is always available, rented equipment might not be available when it is needed.

The B2B Vehicle Rental Industry In this thesis, we consider B2B vehicle rental businesses. In these businesses, commercial customers need to transport cargo and for this reason they order vehicles from a cargo logistics company. The vehicles are e.g. trucks, containers, or rail cars. The logistics rental company provides the vehicles and the customer uses them to store and transport the cargo. Some rental companies only provide the rental service and the transportation service is performed by other companies. This is, for example, the case in the container rental industry. Other rental companies, such as some rail cargo companies, also provide the transportation services. In this case, the company rents out the vehicles and the customer specifies when and where the vehicle should be transported after the cargo has been loaded.

The market value and the market size of the B2B vehicle rental industry is

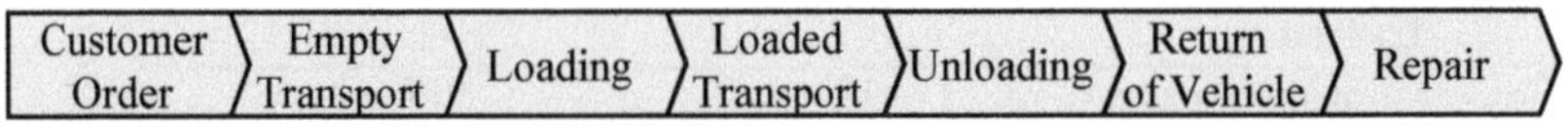

Figure 1.1: Typical rental process for cargo vehicles

large. The total annual market value of the container rental, the rail car rental, and the truck rental industry in Europe in 2005 was about 4,375 mio. Euros. Their total fleet size exceeded 1.5 million vehicles. The detailed numbers per industry are given in Table 1.1.

The operations of vehicle rental companies differ from operations of other transportation service providers, such as airlines or package delivery companies. The distinguishing feature of vehicle rental businesses is that customers of these businesses rent whole vehicles instead of some space in a transportation vehicle.

In this thesis, we focus on rental systems that serve commercial customers. We specialize on rental systems that serve commercial customers, because commercial customers and private customers behave differently and the customer behavior affects the rental system. One example for a difference between commercial and private customers is that private customers typically order only one vehicle while commercial customers often request multiple vehicles in one order.

A typical rental process begins with the customer order and ends when the vehicle becomes available for other customers (we do not consider secondary activities such as billing). When a customer order arrives, the rental company decides what vehicles it will use to fill the order. The empty vehicles are transported from their current location to the customer destination. After the customer has received the vehicles, she loads the cargo into the vehicles and the transportation to the destination location begins. At the destination, the vehicles are unloaded. In some scenarios, the vehicles are loaded again at the same location and are sent to another destination. After the final unloading, the customer informs the rental company, which picks up the vehicles from the customer site. If the vehicles are defect or need to be cleaned, they are brought to a service facility for repair or cleaning. Afterwards, the vehicles become available for subsequent rental services. This generic rental process is summarized in Figure 1.1.

1.3 Modeling Rental Systems as Stochastic Systems

The models analyzed in Chapters 2, 3, 4, and 5 share some common characteristics. In this section, we first define a generic modeling framework for describing and comparing rental models. Afterwards, we introduce rental systems by applying one of the most basic stochastic loss models, the Erlang Loss Model (ELM), to rental systems. In Section 1.4, we use the framework and the ELM to compare the different models presented in this thesis.

The Modeling Framework The rental company possesses a number of vehicles with which it performs the rental services. Vehicles of the same type are grouped into fleets, and the grouping of vehicles into different fleets is known as the *fleet structure*. The number of vehicles in one fleet is referred to as the *fleet size*. In most models, the vehicles are assumed to be *homogeneous*, i.e., they all have identical operating characteristics and the customer has no preference what vehicle of the fleet she receives. However, some approaches allow for *heterogeneous vehicles*, e.g. models with vehicles that have different processing times. For owning and maintaining a car, it is commonly assumed that the rental company has fixed holding costs per time unit and car. These costs may comprise cost of capital, depreciation, and maintenance cost.

Customers may come from *one customer class* or *multiple customer classes.* Customers place orders for rental services at individual times on a continuous time axis. The arrival times of orders are stochastic and so they are not known to the rental company in advance. The rental company only knows the *distribution of order arrivals.* In most rental models, Poisson distributed orders are assumed. However, there are also models in which no distribution assumption is made for the demand. A customer order may require one or more cars for service. When more than one car is required, the number of cars used for one order is referred to as a *batch* and models that allow customer orders with more than one vehicle are *batch-arrival models.* If customer orders of size one are assumed, the model is referred to as a *single-arrival model.* A typical assumption is that customers need the vehicles right away, although we discuss a model in Part 5 where customers place orders a certain time before their actual demand. This is referred to as *advance demand information* (ADI).

For each customer order, the rental company has to decide how many of the ordered vehicles it allocates to the order. The rental company is free to allocate fewer vehicles than required. The policy with which the rental company allocates vehicles to customers is the *admission policy.* If demand is rejected, we assume that it is lost, i.e., it does neither wait nor return at a later time. The quality of the rental service is measured as the fraction of demand filled, which we refer to as the *service level.* There are two possible scenarios concerning customer behavior: Customers may require that their complete order is served (*entire batch blocking (EBB)*) or they may accept partial service (*partial batch blocking (PBB)*). For each rented vehicle, the customer pays a certain price, and this price may depend on the customer class. In some models, customers receive a compensation for each ordered vehicle that is not served.

If a vehicle is assigned to a customer order, the customer receives the car and uses it for a certain period of time, the *rental time.* One main characteristic of our models is that we do not model the rental process itself. We neither explicitly model what the customer is doing with the vehicle during the rental time nor how the transportation service is performed. For our purposes, it is only relevant how long the customer uses the vehicle and when she returns it. Rental times are, as well as customer arrival times, stochastic. Thus, they are not known in advance to the rental company. Some models assume exponential *rental time distributions*, while other models allow for general service time distributions. If customer orders comprise multiple vehicles, the question arises whether the rental times of vehicles

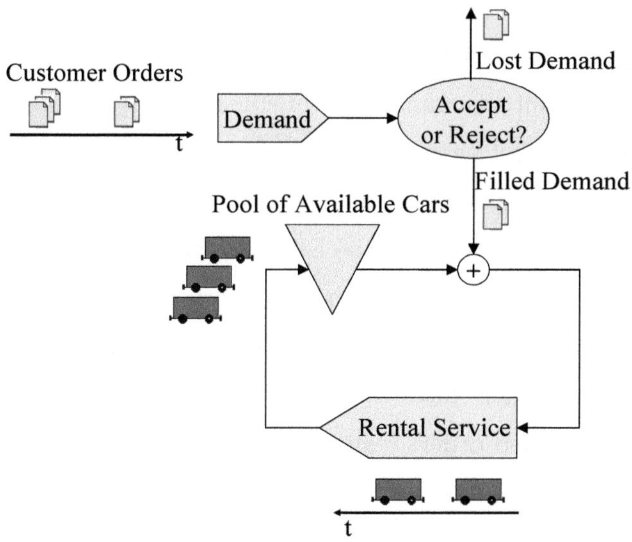

Figure 1.2: Basic rental model

from the same order are *independent* or *dependent.* After a customer has returned the vehicle, it becomes available again and may be used for other customers.

We also distinguish between *stationary* and *non-stationary* models. Stationary models assume that interarrival times and rental times always have the same distribution. In non-stationary models, inter-arrival times and rental times might have different distributions at different times. One common non-stationary model is one that uses demand affected by seasonality. A generic rental model as described above is visualized in Figure 1.2.

The objective function of rental models could be, among others, maximization of expected profit or achieving a certain service level with minimal expected cost. Profit consists of the holding costs, the revenues, and the compensations paid for unfilled demand. In this thesis, we use the fleet size, the fleet structure, and the admission policy in models with multiple customer classes as decision variables.

A Basic Stochastic Rental Model Planning a rental system like the one that we have introduced in this section is not trivial. Since both, customer arrival times and rental times, are stochastic, deterministic planning is not adequate. The stochastic distributions and the decisions that depend on the state of the rental system have to be taken into account simultaneously. We illustrate this complexity by describing one of the most basic stochastic models, the Erlang Loss Model. The model itself has been developed by Erlang (1918). Tainiter (1964) has first applied it to the analysis of rental systems. In the ELM, the rental company has a fleet of c homogeneous vehicles. Each vehicle has holding costs h per time unit. Customers from one common class arrive according to a single-arrival Poisson process with mean λ per time unit. Orders have to be filled as soon as the demand is known, i.e., there are no ADI. Filled orders lead to revenue r, unfilled orders cost penalty p. Rental times are assumed to be independent with an arbitrary distribution. The average rental time is denoted by $\overline{S}$.

The model can be analyzed with Markov Chain Theory (for details see Wolff (1989)). It can be shown that the service level SL of such a system is given by the formula

$$SL = 1 - \frac{\frac{(\lambda\overline{S})^c}{c!}}{\sum\limits_{i=0}^{c} \frac{(\lambda\overline{S})^i}{i!}}. \tag{1.1}$$

Expected profit Π consists of expected revenues $r\lambda SL$, penalties $p\lambda(1 - SL)$, and holding costs hc. In total, expected profit is

$$\Pi = r\lambda SL - p\lambda(1 - SL) - hc. \tag{1.2}$$

If we want to optimize the fleet size, we can vary it until we find the fleet size that brings the most expected profit. Consider an example with $\lambda = 10$ cars/day, $\overline{S} = 7$ days, $r = 150$ Euros per rental, $p = 250$ Euros per loss, and $h = 3,500$ Euros per year. Figure 1.3 shows how expected daily profit depends on the fleet size. The optimal fleet size, based on the figure, would be 82 vehicles with an expected daily profit of 646 Euros. If we had ignored stochasticity and used deterministic planning, we would probably have found a fleet size of $\lceil\lambda\overline{S}\rceil = 70$ to be optimal,

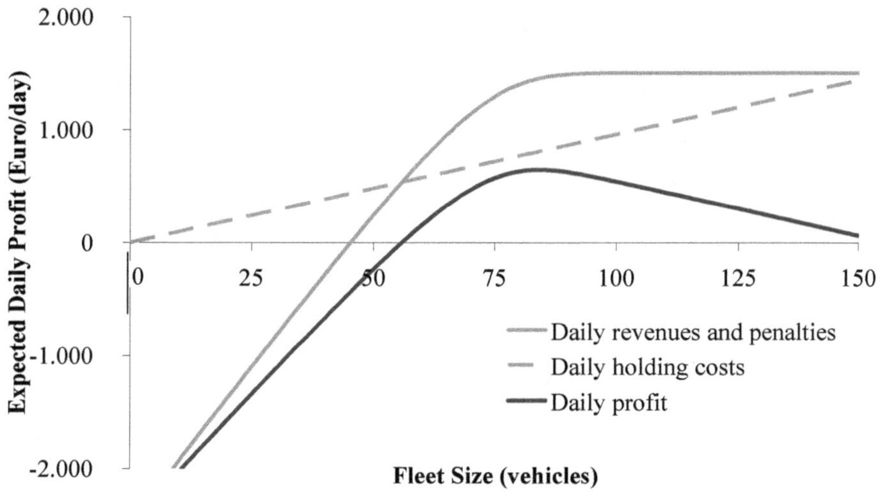

Figure 1.3: Expected daily profit by fleet size for ELM with sample data

which satisfies all demands in a deterministic setting. Expected profit with $c = 70$ is 470 Euros per day, which is 27% below optimality.

The ELM demonstrates that analysis of stochastic rental systems is complex and that ignoring stochasticity in rental systems planning leads to results which are far from optimality.

1.4 Outline

In this section, we describe the structure of the thesis. We explain why there are different, mostly independent research parts, and we give a short outlook into every part. Finally, we compare the four parts by highlighting the differences in the decision variables, the objective functions, and the model assumptions by using the framework defined in Section 1.3.

The remainder of this thesis consists of four separate parts. Each part represents a separate piece of research and is presented in the form of a separate essay. The parts share a general structure. Firstly, there is an introduction which motivates the problem, describes the situation, and outlines the subsequent research. Secondly, each part contains a literature review which provides an in-depth review of the corresponding literature on which the research builds. Thirdly, the model with its assumptions, its decision variables, and its objective function is described. Afterwards, in the main body of each part, the corresponding model is analyzed and optimized. Each analysis and optimization is followed by a short conclusion. The last section of each part contains the mathematical proofs of the analytic results derived in the previous sections.

Finally, after the four main chapters, we conclude the thesis in Chapter 6. In the conclusion, we summarize the key results, give a critical review of the modeling framework that we use for the analysis, and provide an outlook into further research.

We have decided to use such a structure for the thesis, because it facilitates publication of the individual chapters as separate articles in research journals. In addition, it allows the reader to jump directly to one chapter and to read it independently from the others. A disadvantage of this structure is that the literature review sections and the sections containing the model descriptions might overlap at some points.

Next, we give a short outlook into the contents and results of each of the four main chapters.

Chapter 2 Chapter 2 has been motivated by the problem of fleet optimization, which is faced by the rail cargo company that motivated our research. The company operates a fleet of more than 100,000 rail cars and it invests annually significant amounts of money into new cars. Therefore, planning such a fleet is an important activity at the company. In this chapter, we develop and solve analytical models for fleet planning. We first describe the corresponding rental model. We then develop a profit function and derive several structural results, such as the concavity of the profit function in the fleet size. Building on these structural results we show how the fleet size, the fleet structure (i.e., the types of cars being used), and a joint fleet of owned and leased cars can be optimized. Since some of the optimal methods are difficult to implement, we also develop and test an approximation that is easy to implement. To illustrate our findings and to validate our approach, we provide numerical results that are based on real company data.

Chapter 3 In Chapter 3, we consider a fairly general stochastic rental system with arbitrary batch arrival processes, arbitrary service time distributions, and an arbitrary dependence within orders. In the first part of the analysis, we analytically prove convexity of the loss probability in the fleet size for the case with PBB and we show by counterexample that convexity fails when EBB is assumed. In the second part of the analysis, we extend the model to heterogeneous servers. We extend the convexity proof to this model, and we show that the intuitive idea of ordering the servers by decreasing speed is not necessarily optimal under our model assumptions.

Chapter 4 In Chapter 4, we analyze service differentiation. Service differentiation is an emerging method to improve profit and to better serve high-priority customers. It has recently been introduced by the rail cargo company. Customers of this company can choose between classic and premium service. Premium service is priced above classic service and premium customers receive a service guarantee which classic customers do not receive. The company has to decide under which conditions it will ration its fleet capacity to classic customers in order to increase service of premium customers. We model such a situation as a batch-arrival queuing loss system. We describe the model, solve it optimally, and further analyze it by performing numerical experiments based on real company data. We show that the potential of capacity rationing can be substantial in situations like the one we analyzed. We also derive conditions under which rationing is especially beneficial, such as under high unit fleet holding costs or in the presence of batch arrivals compared to single arrivals.

Chapter 5 In Chapter 5 we analyze service differentiation under advance demand information (ADI). We present a stochastic model of a rental system with

	ELM	Ch. 2	Ch. 3	Ch. 4	Ch. 5
Model features					
Allows for heterogeneous cars			✓		
Number of customer classes	1	1	1	2	2
Order arrival distribution	*Poi.*	*Poi.*	*Arb.*	*Poi.*	*Poi.*
Allows for batch arrivals		✓	✓	✓	
Allows for ADI					✓
EBB or PBB	*n/a*	*PBB*	*both*	*PBB*	*n/a*
Rental time distribution	*Arb.*	*Arb.*	*Arb.*	*Ex.*	*Ex.*
Dependent rental times	*n/a*	✓	✓		*n/a*
Allows for non-stationarity		✓			
Objective function					
Expected profit	✓	✓		✓	✓
Service level			✓		
Decision variables					
Fleet size	✓	✓	✓	✓	
Fleet structure		✓			
Admission policy				✓	✓

Arb. = Arbitrary, Ex. = Exponential, n/a = not applicable, Poi. = Poisson

Table 1.2: Characteristics of the ELM and the models of the four main chapters

two customer classes. As in Chapter 4, customers can choose between premium and classic service. However, under premium service, customers also provide ADI by reserving cars ahead of the time when they need them. The company must again decide which demands to fill and which to reject. We model the system and prove that the optimal admission policy is a threshold policy. Since computing the parameters of the policy is computationally intractable, we propose an ADI policy that can be implemented and executed with moderate effort. We analyze the performance of our ADI policy by analytically deriving upper and lower bounds on the optimal expected profit and by performing numerical experiments using company data. The numerical experiments indicate that the potential benefit of using ADI is significant and that our ADI policy performs close to optimal.

The models analyzed in the four chapters all differ at some points in the decision variables, the objective functions, or the model assumptions. Next, we describe the models with the general modeling framework that we have developed in Section 1.3. This allows an easy comparison of the model characteristics. We also contrast the models to the ELM introduced in Section 1.3. The characteristics of the four models and the ELM are given in Table 1.2. It can be seen that all four models extend the ELM in some respects. However, the models among themselves are not necessarily related. The first two models assume one customer class, while the last two models assume two customer classes. Therefore, the first two models could have more general assumptions about the underlying operations, such as dependent rental times within orders. Each model has a different focus, and with each model we have tried to make only the most essential assumptions with which the models become analytically tractable. The model assumptions are described in detail in each of the four main chapters.

Chapter 2

Fleet Sizing and Fleet Structuring under Batch Arrivals

2.1 Introduction

Cargo logistics providers invest major sums into their moving assets. In the U.S. and Europe alone, sales of locomotives, rail cars, containers, trucks, and trailers exceeded 25 billion Euros in 2002 (see U.S. Census Bureau (2005) and European Communities (2006)). Since the moving assets of a logistics provider account for a large fraction of the total assets and since the moving assets determine to a large extent the service level a company can offer, proper management of the moving assets is crucial. In this chapter, we analyze several key aspects that address the optimal management of moving assets.

Our research was motivated by an optimization problem we faced at one of the largest European rail cargo companies. The company operates a fleet of more than $100,000$ rail cars with an average price of over $50,000$ Euros per rail car. The company decides regularly on the fleet size, fleet structure, and fleet leasing. The *fleet size* refers to the total number of cars the company operates. The *fleet structure* describes what types of cars the company operates. *Fleet leasing* is an option whereby rail cars can be leased from specialized companies on a medium-term basis. Traditionally, these decisions were made by the company with very

F. Papier, *Optimization of Rental Systems*, Edition KWV,
https://doi.org/10.1007/978-3-658-24313-5_2

limited use of mathematical models and the company wondered if it could improve its decision making by using more advanced mathematical models. To answer this question, we develop analytical models that take the stochastic nature of the rental business into account. In this chapter, we present these models and report numerical results.

The focus of our research is on the development and solution of *analytical models* for fleet sizing and structuring and on the derivation of *structural properties* of the optimal solutions. The contribution is twofold. Firstly, we develop and solve analytical models that extend the literature on rental fleet optimization. Unlike previous literature, we take demand and rental time uncertainty, seasonality, and order batching simultaneously into account and make very few assumptions on the rental time distributions. Secondly, we present numerical results that are based on data of the company that motivated this research and report on the implementation of our model.

The remainder of this chapter is organized as follows: In Section 2.2, we review the relevant literature. In Section 2.3, we develop the rental model, prove the concavity of the profit function, and show how optimal fleet sizes can be computed. In Section 2.4, we show how the fleet structure can be optimized. In Section 2.5, we analyze how companies can take optimal advantage of fleet leasing by using their own fleet for covering the base demand and leasing cars for covering peak demands. In Section 2.6, we present an approximation for our model that is very easy to implement. In Section 2.7, we compare our model to a very detailed simulation model of the operations at the cargo rail company that motivated our research. In addition, we describe the implementation of our model at the cargo rail company and report on how the analytical methods facilitate decision making. In Section 2.8, we conclude. We provide numerical data for all theoretical results. All proofs are contained in Section 2.9.

2.2 Literature Review

Two lines of research are relevant for fleet sizing and structuring. The first line of research is on queuing models, the second line of research on time and space models. The objectives, levels of detail, and generality of the results that can be derived by these two types of models are quite different and we describe them briefly next. Then, we review the related literature in queuing systems for rental systems and time and space models.

Queuing Models vs. Time and Space Models Queuing models are used for long-term decision making, such as planning fleet sizes and fleet structures over the next years. They neglect various details of the underlying system, such as the spatial structure of the network, and rely on aggregate demand and rental time data. The resulting models are analytically tractable and therefore quite general properties of the models can be derived. Based on these properties, efficient optimization algorithms can be developed and structural insights can be derived.

However, for operational short-term decision making, such as determining the assignment of cars to demands over the next days, queuing models are not appropriate and time and space models are the appropriate choice. Time and space models consider the underlying system on a very detailed level. They build on detailed demand and rental time data to determine the assignment of cars to demands. Since the resulting models are complex, only medium-size problems can be solved optimally and large-size problems are typically solved heuristically. Time and space models can also be used for long-term fleet sizing and structuring. However, this requires the modeler to estimate quite detailed future demand and rental time data and to implement a complex model with a long run time.

Queuing Models for Rental Systems Tainiter (1964) was the first to apply queuing models to rental systems. He shows the correspondence between service systems and loss systems and derives expressions for expected profits under renewal arrivals and exponential service times. Koenigsberg and Lam (1976) develop a model based on cyclic queues with backorders to analyze the special case of gas vessels shuttling between two sea ports. Their objective is to analyze the effect of the fleet size on the mean delay time in a vessel cycle. Parikh (1977) uses a queuing model for modeling rail car rental systems. He uses an $M/G/c$ queue with backorders to determine the steady state distribution of the number of rail cars in use. He determines the optimal fleet size and structure under a service level constraint. Turnquist and Jordan (1986) address the fleet sizing problem for a container network. Their model assumes deterministic demand but allows for stochastic transportation times. Du and Hall (1997) approach the fleet sizing problem from an inventory theory perspective. The authors analytically derive optimal fleet sizes and a method of balancing empty and loaded flows in a transportation network.

Altman et al. (2001) analyze admission controls for queuing loss systems with multiple customer classes. Savin et al. (2005) extend the results of Altman et al., model a loss system with two customer classes, and apply their model to the optimization of rental systems. They assume Poisson arrivals and exponentially distributed service times. The focus of their research is on revenue management, but they also analyze fleet sizing. Örmeci and Burnetas (2005) also analyze a loss system with two customer classes and exponentially distributed service times. They allow for compound Poisson arrivals and assume that the service times of customers from the same order are independent. The focus of their research is on admission policies and the development of optimal thresholds for both classes. Gans and Savin (2007) develop a model for rental businesses with two customer classes: contract customers and walk-in customers. They assume Poisson arrivals and exponential service times which are identical for both types of customers. Their objective is to find optimal admission control for contract customers and optimal prices for walk-in customers.

Time and Space Models Time and space models are network models, which explicitly consider the interdependence between time periods and between locations in a transportation network. A large part of this research is devoted to fleet operations. Articles on fleet operations concentrate on finding an optimal allocation of demand and transportation capacity in a transportation network. This problem is known as the Dynamic Fleet Management Problem (DFMP). Among the first attempts to solve the fleet allocation problem in a stochastic setting are Jordan and Turnquist (1983) and Powell (1986). Since this time, many articles have extended the results on solving fleet operations problems. Some authors developed more efficient solution algorithms, such as the SLAP heuristic (cf. Frantzeskakis and Powell (1990)), Logistics Queuing Networks (cf. Powell et al. (1995) and Powell and Carvalho (1998)), or the CAVE algorithm (cf. Godfrey and Powell (2002a), and Godfrey and Powell (2002b)). Progress has also been made in extending the level of detail of DFMPs, such as substitution between vehicle types (cf. Topaloglu and Powell (2006)). Good overviews of this research area on fleet management can be found in Crainic and Laporte (1998) and Barnhart and Laporte (2007).

Another area of research deals with using time and space models for strategic decision making, such as fleet sizing. Sherali and Tuncbilek (1997) develop a dynamic fleet sizing model for seasonal but deterministic demand. List et al. (2003) formulate a stochastic programming problem for determining the optimal fleet size under uncertainty in the demand, transportation times, and other future operating characteristics. However, their model is computationally intractable for large problems.

Recently developed time and space models focus on integrating strategic and tactical fleet management decisions. Beaujon and Turnquist (1991), Bojovic (2002), and Wu et al. (2005) describe models which explicitly stress the interdependence between fleet sizing and fleet operations. King and Topaloglu (2006) present a model which jointly optimizes prices and fleet operations of a freight carrier fleet.

In this chapter, we extend the research on queuing models for sizing and structuring rental fleets. The first extension is that we relax two assumptions of previous research: We allow for batch arrivals and seasonality of the demand. The second extension is that we obtain more general results than previous research. We derive an analytical expression for the service level and the profit function and prove the concavity of the profit function. This allows us to solve the model optimally and efficiently. We also derive several structural results, such as conditions under which merging fleets is always beneficial.

2.3 Rental Model and Fleet Optimization

In this section, we develop and solve an analytical model for fleet size optimization. We describe our rental system in detail and show how the expected profit can be modeled. We show how the optimal fleet size can be computed under stationary and under non-stationary demand. Building on this result, we analyze the expected profit function and prove that it is concave in the fleet size.

2.3.1 Model Description

The rental system we analyze is based on the cargo operations at one of the largest European cargo rail companies and is typical for cargo logistics providers. The rental process starts with a customer who orders a certain number of cars for transportation of cargo from an origin to a destination. If enough cars are available, the entire order of cars is delivered to the origin. If fewer cars than ordered are available, all cars that are available are delivered to the origin. Excess demand is lost to the cargo logistics provider and customers rent cars from other rental companies or use trucks. After the cars have been delivered to the origin, they are loaded and transported to the destination. At the destination, they are unloaded and become available to meet new demands. We refer to the total time the car is used to fill a customer order as rental time S. Because the cars of an order are usually transported together, the rental times for all cars of the same order are identical. We use a compound Poisson distribution with demand rate λ and a geometric order quantity distribution with mean q to model demand. These distributions fit the empirical demand distributions of the company quite well and they allow us to derive an analytical expression for the profit function.

Our objective is determining the fleet size that maximizes expected profit. Expected profit consists of three components: Expected contribution, expected lost sales cost, and fleet ownership cost.

Expected contribution Let r denote the unit contribution margin, i.e., the difference between unit revenues and unit variable cost. Since the expected demand is λq, the expected contribution margin would be $r\lambda q$ if all demands could be filled. However, since demand is stochastic, not all demands can be filled. Let $\beta(c)$ denote the fraction of demand that is lost with a fleet size of c cars. Then, $(1-\beta(c))$ is the fraction of demand filled and we can compute the expected contribution margin as $r\lambda q(1-\beta(c))$.

Expected lost sales cost If a demand cannot be filled, we charge a penalty cost of p in addition to the lost contribution margin. Depending on the car type, this cost may include a compensation for the customer or additional expenses for the emergency rental of an additional car from an outside company. Since expected demand is λq and the fraction of demand that is not filled is $\beta(c)$, the expected lost sales cost is $p\lambda q\beta(c)$.

Fleet ownership cost We denote the ownership cost of a car by h. It includes depreciation, cost of capital, and the cost of maintenance. With a fleet size of c, fleet ownership cost is hc.

The expected profit is equal to the expected contribution minus expected lost sales cost and fleet ownership cost:

$$\begin{aligned}\Pi(c) &= r\lambda q(1-\beta(c)) - p\lambda q\beta(c) - hc \\ &= r\lambda q - (r+p)\lambda q\beta(c) - hc. \qquad (2.1)\end{aligned}$$

To compute the expected profit, we must compute the fraction of demand lost, $\beta(c)$. We will use the analogy between rental systems and queuing systems to do so. The rental time of the rental system corresponds to the service time of a queuing system, the customer demand per time unit corresponds to the demand rate, and the number of cars corresponds to the number of servers. So, our rental model corresponds to an $M^X/G/c/c$ queue. In queuing theory terms, $\beta(c)$ is referred to as the blocking probability. Theorem 2.1 states how the blocking probability can be computed. The proof of this theorem and all other proofs are contained in Section 2.9.

Theorem 2.1 *The blocking probability of an $M^X/G/c/c$ queue with a geometric order size distribution that is truncated at zero, i.e., with distribution function*

$$f(n) = \frac{1}{q}\left(\frac{q-1}{q}\right)^{n-1}, \quad n > 0, \tag{2.2}$$

is

$$\beta(c) = 1 - \frac{\left(\sum\limits_{k=0}^{c} kg(k)\right) + c(q-1)g(c)}{\lambda q\overline{S}\left(G(c) + (q-1)g(c)\right)}, \tag{2.3}$$

where $g(k) = e^{-\lambda\overline{S}}\sum_{a=0}^{k}\frac{(\lambda\overline{S})^a}{a!}f^{a*}(k)$ denotes the pdf and $G(c) = \sum_{a=0}^{c} g(a)$ the cdf of a compound Poisson distribution and $f^{a*}(k)$, the a-fold convolution of $f(k)$, is given by

$$f^{a*}(k) = \begin{cases} \frac{(k-1)!}{(a-1)!(k-a)!}\left(\frac{1}{q-1}\right)^a\left(\frac{q-1}{q}\right)^k & , \; k \geq a, \\ 0 & , \; k < a. \end{cases} \tag{2.4}$$

From Equation (2.3) it can be seen that the blocking probability depends on the expected rental time $\bar{S}$, but not on higher moments of the rental time. For applications of the formula to rental systems this implies that it suffices to estimate, besides the demand rate and expected order quantities, the expected rental times to compute the exact blocking probability. These data are typically readily available and can be relatively easily predicted for future time periods. Therefore, exact blocking probabilities can be quite easily estimated for rental systems like the one we consider. Fakinos and Sirakoulis (1989) have shown that this result holds for loss systems like ours in general if and only if demand is compound Poisson distributed and order sizes have either a geometric distribution or a geometric lattice distribution.

2.3.2 Performance under Stationary Demand

In Theorem 2.1, we have derived an expression for the blocking probability. Using the expression in the profit function, i.e., with Equation (2.3) in Equation (2.1), we can compute expected profit. Our objective is finding the fleet size c that maximizes expected profit. To guarantee the optimality of the solution, we prove the concavity of the profit function: Theorem 2.1, which is of some interest in its own rights, states that the blocking probability is convex in the fleet size. Since the blocking probability enters the expected profit function with a negative sign, this implies that the expected profit function is concave in the fleet size and we can use any standard optimization approach to find the optimal fleet size efficiently.

Theorem 2.2 *The blocking probability of an $M^X/G/c/c$ queue as described above which is defined by Equation (2.3) is (non-strictly) decreasing and (non-strictly) convex in c.*

Note that the concavity result is not strict and therefore the optimal fleet size might not be unique. We choose the smallest optimal fleet size as our solution and denote it by c^*. It can be computed as

$$\begin{aligned} c^* &= \min\left[c \mid \Pi(c+1) - \Pi(c) \leq 0\right] \\ &= \min[c \mid (r\lambda q - h(c+1) - (r+p)\lambda q\beta(c+1)) \\ &- (r\lambda q - hc - (r+p)\lambda q\beta(c)) \leq 0] \\ &= \min\left[c \mid \Delta\beta(c) \geq -\frac{h}{(r+p)\lambda q}\right], \end{aligned} \tag{2.5}$$

where $\Delta\beta(c) = \beta(c+1) - \beta(c)$.

We can obtain structural insight into the optimal solution. By analyzing Equation (2.5) we can determine the effect of the parameter values on the optimal fleet size: The right hand side of the equation is decreasing in h and increasing in r

Parameters	Non-GPS	GPS
λ [*orders/day*]	2.6	0.9
q [*cars/order*]	20.9	18.6
$\overline{S}$ [*days*]	12.7	16.4
h [*Euro/year*]	4,500	4,700
r [*Euro*]	300	550
p [*Euro*]	250	250
$\widetilde{c}$ [*cars*]	691	275
c^* [*cars*]	873	382

Table 2.1: Operational parameters for two types of bulk goods rail cars

and p. Since $\beta(c)$ is decreasing and convex in c, $\Delta\beta(c)$ is negative and increasing in c (all effects hold non-strictly). Therefore, we can conclude that the optimal fleet size c^* is decreasing in the ownership cost of a car h and increasing in the contribution margin r and the penalty cost p.

We illustrate the application of the model using sanitized sample data of two car types of the rail cargo company. Both car types are used for bulk goods, such as coal or gravel. The difference between the types is that type 2 is equipped with a global positioning system (GPS) and type 1 is not. The current fleet consists of several hundred cars of each type. The parameter data and performance measures of both car types are presented in Table 2.1. All cost and profit data are given in Euro. In our example, the penalty costs are based on the cost of substituting a rail car by truck.

Figure 2.1 shows how the expected profit depends on the fleet size. With optimal fleet sizes, the expected daily profits are $\Pi_1(873) = 3,817$ Euros and $\Pi_2(382) = 3,158$ Euros, respectively. From the graphs we can see that the expected profits are quite sensitive to the fleet size. Thus, using an optimal or close-to-optimal fleet size is important.

In the rental industry it is common practice to plan fleet sizes based on averages. With an average-based calculation, the fleet size $\widetilde{c}$ is computed as

$$\widetilde{c} = \left\lceil \lambda q \overline{S} \right\rceil . \tag{2.6}$$

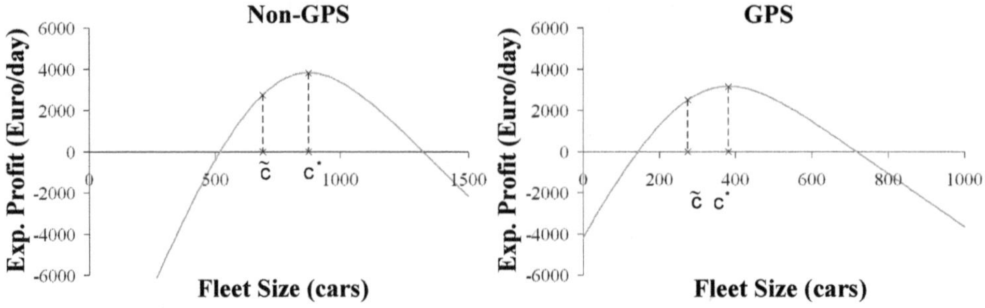

Figure 2.1: Expected daily profit by fleet size of the non-GPS fleet and the GPS fleet

If in our example fleet sizes $\widetilde{c}_1$ and $\widetilde{c}_2$ from the average-based approach were used, they would result in daily expected profits of $\Pi_1(691) = 2,750$ Euros and $\Pi_2(275) = 2,499$ Euros, which are 28.0% and 20.9% below the optimal profits. These results show that it is important to take the stochasticity of the demand and rental time into account when optimizing the fleet size. Next, we discuss how to compute the performance of our rental system under non-stationary demand.

2.3.3 Performance under Non-Stationary Demand

So far, we have analyzed models under stationary demand. However, in our application as well as in many other situations the demand distributions are not stationary but time-dependent. For instance, the demand for cars that carry bulk gravel decreases significantly during winter when construction work is reduced. On the other hand, demand for cars that carry steel coils decreases during summer when industrial production is reduced during vacations. Therefore, we next develop a model for computing blocking probabilities and expected profit under non-stationary demand.

There are no exact methods for computing the performance of rental systems like ours under non-stationary demand, but several approximation methods have been developed that perform quite well. We refer the interested reader to Alnowibet and Perros (2006) for a survey on commonly used approximations. An

	Type 1		Type 2	
	$\bar{S}_t = 12.7$		$\bar{S}_t = 16.4$	
Season	λ_t	q_t	λ_t	q_t
$t = 1$	1.6	25.0	0.5	20.3
$t = 2$	3.4	20.6	1.4	18.6
$t = 3$	2.8	21.3	1.0	19.8
$t = 4$	2.6	18.5	0.8	16.2

Table 2.2: Parameters per season and car type

approximation that tends to perform well in situations like ours where arrival rates are high relative to service times is the Average Stationary Approximation (ASA) (see Whitt (1991)). The idea of the ASA is straightforward. It calculates the stationary performance of each period and then computes the demand-weighted averages over all periods.

Next, we apply the ASA to estimate the total blocking probability for periods $t = \{1, 2, \ldots, T\}$ for compound Poisson arrivals. T denotes the number of periods in a seasonal cycle. Let λ_t be the demand rate in period t, q_t the average order size in period t, and $\bar{S}_t$ the expected rental time in period t. Then, the ASA for the blocking probability is

$$\widehat{\beta}(c) = \frac{\sum_{t=1}^{T} \lambda_t q_t \beta_t(c)}{\sum_{t=1}^{T} \lambda_t q_t}, \tag{2.7}$$

where $\beta_t(c)$ is computed by Equation (2.3). The corresponding ASA of the expected profit is

$$\hat{\Pi}(c) = \sum_{t=1}^{T} \Pi_t(c) = r \sum_{t=1}^{T} \lambda_t q_t - (r+p) \sum_{t=1}^{T} \lambda_t q_t \beta_t(c) - hc. \tag{2.8}$$

We have analyzed the accuracy of the ASA via simulation. For the two car types analyzed earlier (non-GPS and GPS), we have computed the blocking probabilities with the ASA and have compared them with simulation results. The run times of the simulations were chosen such that the half widths of all 95% confidence intervals were less than 0.05%. The data used in the experiment are summarized in Table 2.2. The results for the blocking probabilities are shown in Table 2.3.

	Type 1			Type 2		
c	Sim.	ASA	ε	Sim.	ASA	ε
100	86.2	86.2	0.0	69.3	69.3	0.0
200	72.8	72.8	0.0	43.8	43.8	0.0
500	36.6	36.6	0.0	5.6	5.8	−0.2
1000	4.1	4.1	0.0	0.0	0.0	0.0
2000	0.0	0.0	0.0	0.0	0.0	0.0
5000	0.0	0.0	0.0	0.0	0.0	0.0
c^*	8.4	8.4	0.0	14.5	14.6	−0.1

Table 2.3: Simulated and approximated blocking probabilities for two car types and different fleet sizes

Column ε shows the error in percentage points. The results indicate that ASA works quite well in our setting, even for fleets with highly fluctuating demand between seasons. Thus, we conclude that ASA is an appropriate approximation for applications like ours.

As can be easily seen, Theorem 2.2 extends to the non-stationary case, because the blocking probabilities in each time period are convex and the sum of convex functions is also convex. Therefore, the expected profit is concave in the fleet size and we can use standard optimization approaches for finding the optimal fleet size.

So far, we have assumed that the fleet structure is given. However, in some situations we can relax this assumption. In our example, it would be possible to equip all cars with GPS and fill demand of GPS and non-GPS cars with a common fleet of GPS cars. Customers who order a non-GPS car would receive a GPS car, but they would not gain access to the GPS system. By denying these customers access to the GPS system, we could ensure that we continue charging different prices for both types of cars after merging the fleets. We next analyze the benefits of merging fleets.

2.4 Fleet Structure

Merging several fleets into one fleet seems intuitively appealing. In a merged fleet, customers access a common pool of cars and we can take advantage of risk pooling. The concept of risk pooling is widely applied in inventory theory, where techniques such as postponement (cf. e.g. Baker et al. (1986)) or component commonality (cf. e.g. Lee (1996)) are used to aggregate safety stocks across different products. As in inventory theory, merging fleets improves the performance of the rental system in many situations. An interesting question is under what conditions fleet merging improves the performance (cf. e.g. Gerchak and Mossman (1992)). To answer this question, we analytically analyze the reduction in lost sales and the improvement in expected profit when merging fleets. To quantify the benefits of a fleet merger, we report numerical results of an application. In addition, we show by counterexample that merging fleets with different order size distributions can be unprofitable, even if rental times are identically distributed.

Most fleets that are candidates for a merger have similar characteristics. They are used for similar products and serve similar customers and therefore frequently have similar order size distributions. We concentrate on merging fleets with identical order size distributions and denote the corresponding change in lost sales by

$$\begin{aligned}
\Delta L &= L_{12} - L_1 - L_2 \\
&= L(\lambda_1 + \lambda_2, \frac{\lambda_1 \overline{S}_1 + \lambda_2 \overline{S}_2}{\lambda_1 + \lambda_2}, c_1 + c_2, q) - L(\lambda_1, \overline{S}_1, c_1, q) - L(\lambda_2, \overline{S}_2, c_2, q) \\
&= (\lambda_1 + \lambda_2)\, q\beta(\lambda_1 \overline{S}_1 + \lambda_2 \overline{S}_2, c_1 + c_2, q) \\
&\quad -\lambda_1 q\beta(\lambda_1 \overline{S}_1, c_1, q) - \lambda_2 q\beta(\lambda_2 \overline{S}_2, c_2, q). \qquad (2.9)
\end{aligned}$$

Note that we denoted the blocking probability as $\beta\left(\lambda\overline{S}, c, q\right)$ and the expected loss rate as $L\left(\lambda, \overline{S}, c, q\right)$. The blocking probability depends only on the product of λ and $\overline{S}$ (see Equation (2.3)). Thus, $\beta\left(\lambda\overline{S}, c, q\right)$ is fully determined by the parameters $\lambda\overline{S}$, c, and q. If two fleets are similar in their rental time requirements, i.e., the means of the rental times are identical ($\overline{S}_1 = \overline{S}_2$), merging these two fleets will always reduce lost sales. This result is formally stated in Theorem 2.3.

Par.	Separate			Merged $c_1 + c_2$	Merged c^*
	Reg. C.	Small C.	Sum/Avg.	Value (Δ)	Value (Δ)
λ	13.1	6.0	19.1	19.1	19.1
q	19.6	19.6	19.6	19.6	19.6
$\overline{S}$	8.9	8.9	8.9	8.9	8.9
h	5,400	5,400	5,400	5,400	5,400
r	250	250	250	250	250
p	150	150	150	150	150
c^*	2,585	1,238	3,823	3,823 (0)	3,702 (−121)
$L(c)$	8.9	6.3	15.2	6.7 (−8.5)	10.6 (3.9)
$\Pi(c)$	22,373	8,550	30,923	34,349 (3,426)	34,594 (245)

Table 2.4: Comparison of expected profits and fleet sizes for the two separated fleets and the combined fleet of steel coil cars

Theorem 2.3 *If we merge two fleets with identical rental time distributions, then*

$$\Delta L = L(\lambda_1 + \lambda_2, \overline{S}, c_1 + c_2, q) - L(\lambda_1, \overline{S}, c_1, q) - L(\lambda_2, \overline{S}, c_2, q) \leq 0. \qquad (2.10)$$

Theorem 2.3 shows that merging fleets with identical rental time means reduces lost sales. This result holds not only for two fleets, but also for an arbitrary number of fleets, because we can apply Theorem 2.3 consecutively.

Next, we report a numerical example from the cargo rail company that motivated this research. An example of fleets with similar rental time means are fleets for transporting steel coils. Currently, the company uses two car types that are essentially identical. Cars of the first fleet are equipped with cavities and bolts to hold regular size steel coils, while the cars of the second fleet have cavities and bolts to fix small size steel coils. For comparatively low upgrading costs, the cars of both types can be equipped with additional facilities to hold both sizes of steel coils.

All parameter values and performance measures of this example are given in Table 2.4. The columns *Reg. Coils* and *Small Coils* contain the optimal solutions of the separated fleets with fleet sizes c_1 and c_2. The column *Sum/Avg.* lists the sum or the average of the columns *Reg. Coils* and *Small Coils* and serves as a benchmark for the merged fleet. The columns for $c_1 + c_2$ list the values and value differences (Δ) if we use a single fleet with size $c_1 + c_2$. It shows that combining the fleets results in a reduction of expected lost sales of 8.5 rentals/day (−55.9 %) and in an increase in daily profits of 3,426 Euros (11.1%). To further improve performance, we optimized the fleet size of the merged fleet. The results of the optimization are shown in columns c^* and show that an optimization leads to an additional increase in expected profit by 245 Euros (0.8%). Since the typical return on sales in the industry is about 3% (see DataMonitor (2003, 2005)), merging fleets can be an important option for improving profitability.

In some cases, the rental times are not identical in the two fleets to be merged. Then, depending on the parameters, the blocking probability of the merged fleet can be closer to the blocking probability of fleet 1 or the blocking probability of fleet 2. We can see from Equation (2.9) that when $\beta(\lambda_1\overline{S}_1 + \lambda_2\overline{S}_2, c_1 + c_2, q)$ approaches $max(\beta(\lambda_1\overline{S}_1, c_1, q), \beta(\lambda_2\overline{S}_2, c_2, q))$, merging does not decrease the loss rate. Thus, merging is not always profitable. We can even state the stronger result that for large differences in the rental time means merging always becomes unprofitable.

Proposition 2.1 *For every parameter constellation of $\lambda_1, c_1, \lambda_2, c_2, q$, there is a difference in rental time means $\overline{S}_2 - \overline{S}_1 > 0$ such that merging fleets is increasing the loss rate for all rental time means with larger difference.*

So far, we have assumed that the merged fleet has a fleet size of $c_1 + c_2$ cars. However, in the long run, the company can again optimize the size of the merged fleet. It is obvious that $\Delta\Pi = \Pi_{12} - \Pi_1 - \Pi_2$ is larger with an optimized fleet size than with $c_1 + c_2$ cars. However, even after an additional optimization of the fleet size the merger can be unprofitable.

Proposition 2.2 *For every parameter constellation of λ_1, λ_2, q and optimal fleet sizes c_1^*, c_2^*, and c_{12}^*, there is a difference in rental time means $\overline{S}_2 - \overline{S}_1 > 0$ such that merging fleets is not beneficial for all rental time means with larger difference.*

The change in profit depends not only on the change in loss rate, ΔL, but also on the cost parameters r and p. Denote the monetary value of lost sales costs by

$\Delta L^{(m)}$. This quantity is given by

$$\begin{aligned}\Delta L^{(m)} &= \frac{(r_1+p_1)\,\lambda_1+(r_2+p_2)\,\lambda_2}{\lambda_1+\lambda_2}L(\lambda_1+\lambda_2,\frac{\lambda_1\overline{S}_1+\lambda_2\overline{S}_2}{\lambda_1+\lambda_2},c_1+c_2,q)\\ &\quad-(r_1+p_1)\,L(\lambda_1,\overline{S}_1,c_1,q)-(r_2+p_2)\,L(\lambda_2,\overline{S}_2,c_2,q). \qquad (2.11)\end{aligned}$$

From Equation (2.11) it follows that merging fleets is beneficial if the lump-sum revenue and penalty cost parameters r and p are proportional to the mean rental time $\overline{S}$. This is a natural condition, because many companies determine these parameters by taking into account the average rental time. Proposition 2.3 states that result.

Proposition 2.3 *Let $(\lambda_1,\overline{S}_1,c_1,q)$ and $(\lambda_2,\overline{S}_2,c_2,q)$ define two rental systems as described in Section 2.3. If $\frac{r_1+p_1}{\overline{S}_1}=\frac{r_2+p_2}{\overline{S}_2}$, it holds that*

$$\Delta L^{(m)} \leq 0 \qquad (2.12)$$

for all $\lambda_1,\lambda_2,\overline{S}_1,\overline{S}_2>0$, $q>1$, and $c_1,c_2\geq 0$.

In the results above, we assumed different mean rental times for the car types to be merged. However, even with identical rental time distributions, merging does not always reduce the loss rate, if the order size means vary (unlike Theorem 2.3). This is because few orders with large order sizes can occupy the merged rental system and, thus, may block many orders with small order sizes. In this case, the availability of cars in the near future will be different between the separate and the merged scenario. Having many small orders in the system rather than one big order is in most situations "better" in terms of future performance and this effect may offset the effect of risk pooling. We give an example for such a setting in Section 2.9 (see Example 2.1).

So far, we have assumed that the company can only employ a fixed fleet of their own cars. Next, we analyze the case in which cars can be leased on a short-term basis to supplement the fleet of owned cars. We show how the performance of the rental system under leasing option can be evaluated and how the fleet size and leasing quantities can be optimized.

2.5 Fleet Leasing

Many rental applications experience significant demand variations across seasons. The seasonal demand variations can be predicted quite well, which opens an interesting optimization approach: We can operate the rental system with a certain number of cars to fill the base demand and lease additional cars for seasons in which demand is high. In this section, we analyze how such a rental system with leasing option can be modeled and optimized. At first, we analyze how the performance of a rental system with owned and leased cars can be evaluated. Afterwards, we demonstrate how to derive the optimal leasing quantity for a given fleet size and how to find the optimal fleet size in the presence of a leasing option.

We denote the cost of leasing one car for one period by v and the number of leased cars over the seasonal cycle by $\mathbf{l} = \{l_1, l_2, \ldots, l_T\}$. The expected profit is

$$\widehat{\Pi}(c, \mathbf{l}) = r \sum_{t=1}^{T} \lambda_t q_t - (r+p) \sum_{t=1}^{T} \lambda_t q_t \beta_t(c + l_t) - hc - v \sum_{t=1}^{T} l_t. \tag{2.13}$$

We assume that $vT > h$. Otherwise, owning cars is not preferable over leasing cars for the entire demand. The optimal number of leased cars can be determined based on Proposition 2.4. The proposition states how $\mathbf{l}^*(c)$, the optimal number of leased cars, can be computed for a given fleet size c.

Proposition 2.4 *For a given fleet size c, the optimal number of leased cars in period t is*

$$l_t^*(c) = \left[\widehat{l_t^*} - c\right]^+, \tag{2.14}$$

where

$$\widehat{l_t^*} = \min \left[\widehat{l} \mid \Delta\beta_t(\widehat{l}) \geq -\frac{v}{(r+p)\, \lambda_t q_t}\right] \tag{2.15}$$

can be interpreted as the optimal fleet size in period t if the ownership cost of a car were v.

Car Type	Without leasing	With leasing				
	c^*	c^*	l_1^*	l_2^*	l_3^*	l_4^*
1	885	740	0	336	189	13
2	400	288	0	262	142	0
3	2571	2,477	114	0	0	270
4	1226	1,124	305	111	0	0

Table 2.5: Comparison of fleet sizes with and without leasing option and leasing quantities

Car Type	Without leasing	With leasing	Improvement
	$\hat{\Pi}(c^*, \bar{\mathbf{0}})$	$\hat{\Pi}(c^*, \mathbf{l}^*)$	$\hat{\Pi}(c^*, \mathbf{l}^*) - \hat{\Pi}(c^*, \bar{\mathbf{0}})$
1	3,056	3,594	538 (17.6%)
2	2,556	3,124	568 (22.2%)
3	21,833	22,073	240 (1.1%)
4	7,851	8,267	416 (5.3%)

Table 2.6: Comparison of expected profits with and without leasing option

Typically, we are interested in the joint optimization of the fleet size c and the number of leased cars $\mathbf{l}$. Therefore, we prove the concavity of $\hat{\Pi}(c, \mathbf{l}^*(c))$ in the fleet size c, which allows us to compute the optimal fleet size and the optimal number of leased cars with standard optimization approaches. The concavity of the expected profit is formally stated in Proposition 2.5.

Proposition 2.5 *The expected profit $\hat{\Pi}(c, \mathbf{l}^*(c))$ is (non-strictly) concave in c.*

We next illustrate the effect of leasing on fleet sizes and expected profits by comparing the optimal solutions for four car types with and without leasing over $T = 4$ seasons. The leasing costs for each car type are $v_1 = 1,250$ Euros, $v_2 = 1,325$ Euros, $v_3 = 1,500$ Euros, and $v_4 = 1,500$ Euros per season and car. All other data are the same as above. The optimal solutions are shown in Table 2.5, the corresponding expected profits and the profit improvements in Table 2.6. The results show that the improvements vary between car types. For car types with high demand variability between seasons (type 1 and type 2) the improvement is much higher than for car types with low variability between seasons (type 3 and type 4). In our numerical experiments, the optimal fleet sizes are smaller with leasing than without leasing. This is what we would expect to hold in general, because without leasing we must use cars of our own fleet for covering all demand, whereas with leasing we can use some leased cars for covering peak demands. That the fleet size is in general smaller with the leasing option than without the leasing option is stated in Proposition 2.6.

Proposition 2.6 *The optimal fleet size c^* is (non-strictly) smaller with leasing than without leasing.*

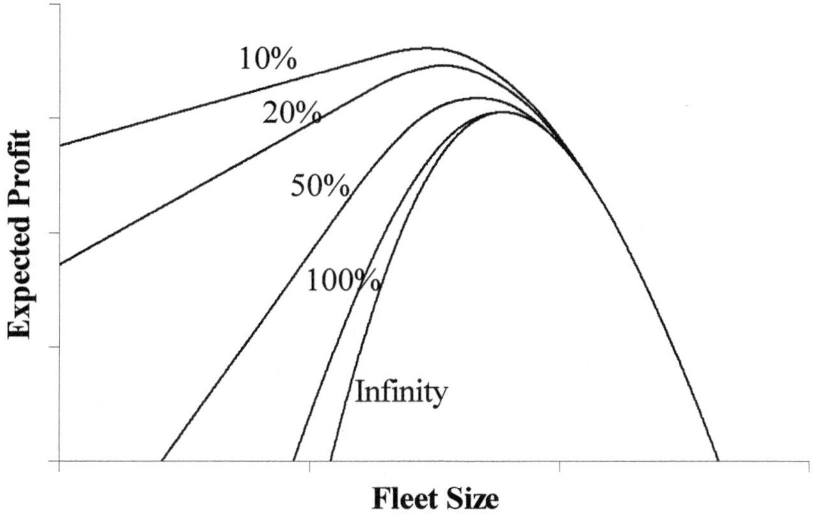

Figure 2.2: Expected profit by fleet size of car type 1 (GPS cars) for different leasing cost rates

The sensitivity of the expected profit with respect to the fleet size is shown in Figure 2.2. In the example, the leasing prices v are 10%, 20%, 50%, 100% above the ownership costs per season $\frac{h}{T}$. The case without leasing option is also included in the graph (denoted by *Infinity*). The graph shows that the expected profit is decreasing in the leasing cost and that the optimal fleet size is increasing in the leasing cost. It also shows that the sensitivity of the expected profit with respect to the fleet size is much higher without the leasing option than with the leasing option, in particular for fleet sizes below the optimum and for low leasing cost.

Next, we derive an approximation which makes our model easy to implement.

		$\frac{\lambda \overline{S} q}{c} = 0.8$		$\frac{\lambda \overline{S} q}{c} = 1.0$		$\frac{\lambda \overline{S} q}{c} = 1.2$	
c	q	Exact	Approx.	Exact	Approx.	Exact	Approx.
200	2.0	1.1%	1.0%	9.1%	9.5%	20.6%	21.3%
500	2.0	0.1%	0.0%	5.9%	6.1%	18.6%	18.9%
1,000	2.0	0.0%	0.0%	4.2%	4.3%	17.7%	17.9%
2,000	2.0	0.0%	0.0%	3.0%	3.1%	17.2%	17.3%
200	5.0	5.9%	5.5%	15.0%	15.7%	24.8%	26.2%
500	5.0	1.6%	1.4%	9.9%	10.2%	21.1%	21.8%
1,000	5.0	0.3%	0.2%	7.2%	7.3%	19.3%	19.7%
2,000	5.0	0.0%	0.0%	5.1%	5.2%	18.1%	18.4%
200	20.0	19.6%	19.6%	27.8%	30.1%	35.1%	38.8%
500	20.0	10.0%	9.5%	19.1%	20.1%	28.0%	29.9%
1,000	20.0	5.0%	4.6%	14.1%	14.6%	24.1%	25.3%
2,000	20.0	1.9%	1.6%	10.3%	10.6%	21.3%	22.1%

Table 2.7: Comparison of exact and approximate blocking probabilities for different traffic intensities, fleet sizes, and mean order sizes

2.6 Easy Approximation

Our optimal solutions are based on Equation (2.3), which computes the exact blocking probability per season in our rental system. However, the formula is not easy to evaluate since it involves computing multiple sums. Thus, programming is usually needed and the computation time requirements can be high if a large number of fleets need to be optimized. Therefore, we develop an approximation for the blocking probability that can be easily evaluated with scientific calculators or spreadsheet software. Proposition 2.7 states how the blocking probability $\beta(c)$ can be approximated.

Proposition 2.7 *The blocking probability $\beta(c)$ can be approximated by*

$$\begin{aligned}\beta(c) \;&\approx\; 1-\frac{\mu\Phi(z(c))-\sigma\phi(z(c))}{\mu\left(\Phi(z(c))+(q-1)\left(\Phi(z(c+\frac{1}{2}))-\Phi(z(c-\frac{1}{2}))\right)\right)}\\ &\quad-\frac{c(q-1)\left(\Phi(z(c+\frac{1}{2}))-\Phi(z(c-\frac{1}{2}))\right)}{\mu\left(\Phi(z(c))+(q-1)\left(\Phi(z(c+\frac{1}{2}))-\Phi(z(c-\frac{1}{2}))\right)\right)},\end{aligned} \tag{2.16}$$

where $z(x) = \frac{x-\mu}{\sigma}$, $\phi(z)$ and $\Phi(z)$ are the pdf and cdf of a standard normal distribution, respectively, and μ and σ are $\mu = \lambda\overline{S}q$ and $\sigma = \sqrt{\lambda\overline{S}q(2q-1)}$.

The approximation is based on approximating the compound Poisson distribution by a normal distribution. Approximation (2.16) is similar to the approximation of a $G/GI/c/0$ loss system under heavy-load developed by Whitt (1984), except for the additional term $(q-1)\left(\Phi(z(c+\frac{1}{2}))-\Phi(z(c-\frac{1}{2}))\right)$ that appears in both the numerator and denominator. Table 2.7 shows the blocking probability for traffic intensities per car $(\frac{\lambda q \overline{S}}{c})$ of 0.8, 1.0, and 1.2, order sizes q of 2.0, 5.0, and 20.0, and fleet sizes c of 200, 500, 1,000, and 2,000. To analyze the performance of the approximation in fleet-sizing applications, we have used Equation (2.16) instead of Equation (2.3) to compute the optimal fleet sizes of the example in Section 2.3. Using the approximation we obtained "optimal" fleet sizes of $\widehat{c}_1^* = 888$ and $\widehat{c}_2^* = 394$. So, the fleet sizes of fleets 1 and 2 are 1.7% and 3.1% above optimality. The corresponding profits $\Pi_1(888) = 3,810$ Euros and $\Pi_2(394) = 3,150$ Euros of these fleet sizes are each 0.2% below optimality. The data illustrate that Approximation (2.16) gives a good estimate of the true blocking probability for a range of parameters typically found in applications like ours. In general, the approximation seems to perform better for smaller values of q than for larger values of q, because the approximation error of using a normal distribution instead of a compound Poisson distribution seems to decrease when the compound Poisson distribution approaches a pure Poisson distribution.

2.7 Model Validation and Implementation

Our models have been implemented at the cargo rail company that motivated our research. The company owns about 100,000 rail cars and transports more than 200 million tons of cargo annually. In this section, we first describe the rental process and the optimization models used by the company. Then, we validate the accuracy of our queuing model by comparing the queuing model with a detailed simulation of the actual system. Finally, we report how the model is being used by the cargo rail company.

2.7.1 Rental Process and Optimization Models

At the cargo rail company, customers place orders with the central sales department. Once a day, the customer service department matches these customer requests with empty rail cars. Cars that are assigned to an order are then transported to the origin, where they are loaded. If the customer has finished loading, she informs the rail company. The rail company then picks up the loaded cars and ships them to the destination. At the destination, the cars are unloaded. In some cases, the rail cars are used by the customer at the destination for a subsequent transport to a second destination. However, in most cases, the cars are returned to the cargo rail company. If necessary, cars are sent to a repair or cleaning facility to be maintained or cleaned. An optimization software performs the daily matching between customer requests and empty cars. This software takes the spatial structure of the network on a detailed level into account to find the redistribution of empty cars that generates the least empty car mileage. It also considers substitution between car types. The software uses a network flow model and solves it with the out-of-kilter algorithm (cf. Fulkerson (1961)) to compute minimal-cost network flows. For details on the implementation of the software see Nievergelt et al. (1970).

The existing software efficiently handles the daily assignment of cars to customer orders. However, fleet planners were looking for a solution for planning fleet sizes, fleet structures, and leasing options over medium and long terms. For instance, they are using a rolling horizon plan over 5 years for planning purchases and disposals for several hundred types of rails cars and update this plan bi-annually. To create robust plans, the planners perform various scenario analyses of the key parameters, such as demand rates and rental times.

Our first approach to support the planning at the company was to develop a simulation model. This simulation model includes detailed information on demands, loading times, unloading times, repair times, cleaning time, etc. for each railway station and contains the network structure and the transportation times between all stations. To assign rail cars to demands, it uses a copy of the out-of-kilter

	Sim. Model	Queuing Model
Features		
Fleet Size	✓	✓
Stochastic Car Cycle Times	✓	✓
Stochastic Demand	✓	✓
Order Batching	✓	✓
Seasonality	✓	✓
Intra-Week Fluctuations	✓	–
Substitution of Car Types	✓	–
Characteristics		
Run time (1 setting and 1 car type)	>1 hour	<1 second
Complexity	high	low
Level of detail	high	low
Number of parameters to estimate	>10,000	12
Model solution	approximate	optimal
General results	no	yes

Table 2.8: Features and characteristics of simulation model and queuing model

algorithm used by the company. The simulation uses estimates of the demand distributions and duration distributions (loading times, repair times, etc.) and considers day-of-the-week and month-of-the-year fluctuations. For details on the simulation model see Weyers (2007).

Initially, we used this simulation model for fleet sizing. However, due to the high level of detail included in the model, the data requirements and run times of the simulation model were quite high. Therefore, the company was looking for an easier-to-handle approach for fleet sizing and we developed the queuing systems presented in this chapter. Table 2.8 compares the main features and characteristics of the simulation model and the queuing model.

The simulation model contains very detailed information on the actual systems and more than 10,000 parameter values must be estimated to simulate a single car type. Due to the high complexity of the simulation model, it models reality quite closely and has a high level of accuracy, but it also has a long run time. We found that many of the details included in the simulation are not required for fleet sizing. For instance, the time-and-space algorithm included in the simulation assigns a specific car to each demand and routes the car optimally through the network. For estimating travel distances and some other performance indicators, this specific routing must be taken into account. However, for fleet sizing, the network structure and the routing play a very minor role: Essentially each demand can be filled within the order lead time if an empty car is available somewhere in the network and transportation time is less than 10% of the total rental time. Therefore, we decided to build a model that contains the most relevant parameters for fleet sizing only. The resulting model that ignores the spatial structure of the network is the one we present in this chapter. Besides a much shorter run time and fewer data requirements than the simulation, the queuing model has two additional advantages over the simulation: Its solution can be proven to be optimal (under the modeling assumptions of the queuing models) and it can be used to prove general results, such as identifying conditions under which merging fleets is always optimal.

2.7.2 Validation of Queuing Model

The queuing model ignores many details of the actual system. To validate the accuracy of the queuing model for fleet size planning, we compare its performance with the performance of the simulation. For the rail car types analyzed in the previous sections, we have simulated the expected profit for various fleet sizes and compare it with the expected profit of the queuing model. For each car type and fleet size, we ran 25 replications, each simulating 3 years of rail car operations. The average run time was 1.8 hours per car type and fleet size on a high-end PC. The results are shown in Figure 2.3. The figure also shows the 95% confidence interval of the simulation. The graphs show that the expected profit estimated by the simulation and the queuing model are quite close. Also, the shapes of the simulated expected profit curves and the expected profit curves of the queuing model are very similar and they obtain their maxima for similar fleet sizes. This is an important observation, because it implies that the queuing model finds similar solutions to the simulation.

To quantify the differences between the optimal fleet sizes determined by the

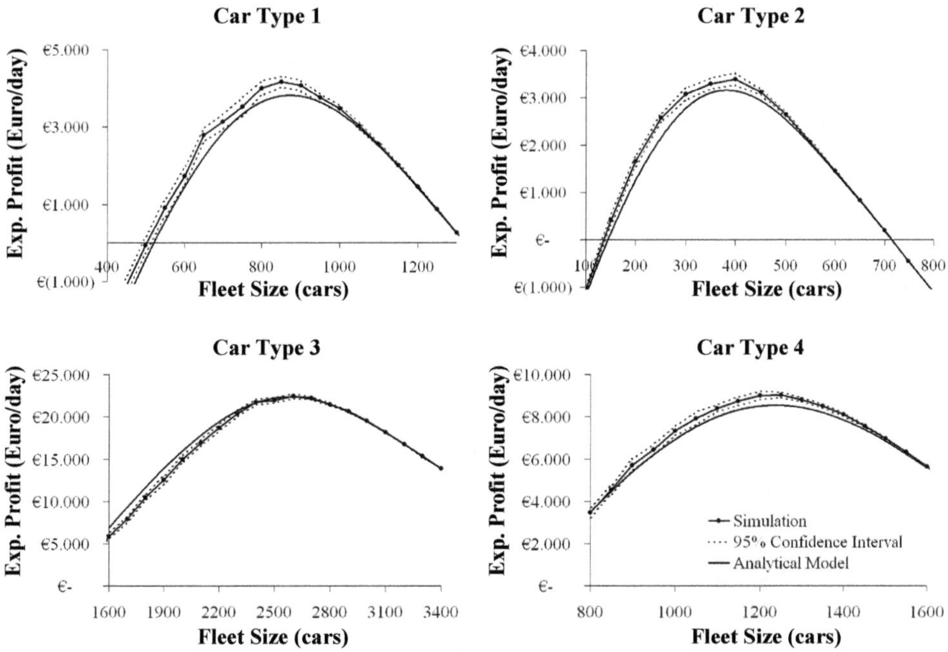

Figure 2.3: Expected profit of simulation model and queuing model

simulation and the queuing model, we have determined optimal fleet sizes with both approaches. The results are shown in Table 2.9. For car type 1, for instance, we varied the fleet sizes in the simulation in steps of 50. From Figure 2.3, we conclude that the optimal fleet size is between 800 and 900. Based on the simulation results we have, we choose $c^*_{Sim} = 850$, where c^*_{Sim} denotes the best fleet size found by the simulation. We denote the corresponding expected profit by $\Pi_{\text{Sim}}(c^*_{\text{Sim}})$. Note that we could decrease the step size of the simulation and increase the simulation length to get more accurate estimates of the expected profit for fleet sizes between 800 and 900. However, this would result in long run times of the simulation and since determining optimal fleet sizes via simulation is not the focus of this thesis we did not perform these experiments. In Table 2.9, we also report the optimal fleet size determined by the queuing model. For car type 1, for instance, we obtain $c^*_{\text{Queue}} = 873$. Using the simulation, we can determine the

Type	c^*_{Sim}	c^*_{Queue}	$\Pi_{\text{Sim}}(c^*_{\text{Sim}})$	$\Pi_{\text{Sim}}(c^*_{\text{Queue}})$	ε
1	850 (±50)	873	4,171 (±140)	4,083 (±166)	−2.1%
2	400 (±50)	382	3,397 (±131)	3,468 (±104)	+2.0%
3	2,600 (±100)	2,585	22,436 (±285)	22,455 (±176)	0.1%
4	1,250 (±50)	1,238	9,032 (±126)	8,997 (±119)	−0.4%

Table 2.9: Optimal fleet size and expected profit of simulation model and queuing model

expected profit if this fleet size were used. We report the corresponding simulated expected profit in column $\Pi_{\text{Sim}}(c^*_{\text{Queue}})$. Column ε shows the percentage deviation between both profits. As Table 2.9 indicates, the optimal fleet sizes obtained by the simulation and the queuing model as well as the expected profits that are achieved by the optimal fleet sizes obtained by the simulation and the queuing model are very similar, which validates the accuracy of our queuing model.

2.7.3 Implementation

The queuing model has been distributed to fleet planners and to selected sales managers. The input data for the models are provided by two departments. The customer service department has access to databases with historical data and provides historical and current values of demand rates, order quantities, and rental times. For many decisions, estimates of future demands and rental times are also relevant. These data are provided by the sales department. The fleet planners and sales managers regularly use the queuing model for decision support:

- *Fleet planners* decide about car purchases and disposals. They use the queuing models presented in Sections 2.3 and 2.5 to decide on the number of cars to purchase and dispose of over the next 5 years and to decide on the number of cars to lease during the next 12 months.

- *Sales managers* negotiate contracts with customers. These contracts include prices, penalty costs, fleet sizes, and availabilities of cars. Some customers prefer to be served by a separate fleet of cars despite the fact that other customers use identical cars. Sales managers use the fleet merging model described in Section 2.4 and sensitivity reports like the ones presented in

Section 2.3 to better understand the impact of fleet splitting and factors on the overall expected profit and use the results of the analyses to determine the terms of the contracts.

- *Fleet planners and sales managers* regularly meet in joint planning sessions in which they plan future fleet sizes and structures. While different alternatives are discussed, agreeing jointly on decisions had often been difficult because the effect of the decisions on service levels and expected profits could not be quantified well. By using the queuing models described in Sections 2.3, 2.4, and 2.5, decision makers are now able to evaluate alternative strategies, especially strategies concerning merging or splitting fleets, changing revenue and cost parameters, and increasing sales better than before.

2.8 Conclusion

In this chapter, we have developed queuing models for fleet sizing, fleet structuring, and fleet leasing. To prove structural results of our queuing model and to derive an optimal solution approach, we proved that the blocking probability is convex in the number of servers, a result that is of some interest in its own rights. Building on this property, we showed that expected profit is concave in the fleet size and hence that the optimal fleet size can be found with any standard optimization approach. We also showed that, depending on the cost structure and the system parameters, merging fleets reduces lost sales and increases expected profit. Finally, we showed that seasonal effects have a significant impact on the average availability of a rental system and that the impact of seasonality on expected profit can be decreased by optimally leasing cars on a seasonal basis. We backed up our analysis by conducting numerical experiments based on data from the rail car rental process of a major European cargo rail company. To demonstrate the accuracy of our queuing model, we compared its performance with the performance of a quite detailed simulation model and showed that the results of the simulation were close to the results of the queuing model.

The results of this chapter can also be used by decision makers of related rental businesses to improve profit by optimizing fleet sizes, fleet merging, and fleet leasing. The approximation formula given in Section 2.6 can easily be used with any scientific calculator or be implemented in spreadsheet software. Furthermore, the monotonicity and concavity results provide decision makers with insight into fundamental relationships within their rental system.

In this chapter, we have studied the case in which the rail company pays a penalty for each unmet demand. Under this assumption, we have demonstrated how to maximize expected profit. However, many companies do not explicitly maximize profit, but minimize cost with a constraint on service. Using a service constraint instead of penalty cost has an important advantage - the monetary effect of lost sales on profits does not have to be estimated. However, an appropriate value for the service level must be specified. Our model can easily be altered to a service level constraint model. If specifying a service level is easier than estimating the cost of lost sales, the optimal fleet size can be computed as

$$c^* = \min \left[c \mid \beta(c) \leq 1 - SL \right], \tag{2.17}$$

where the target service level SL denotes the fraction of demand that can be filled.

The focus of our research is on managing capacity in rental systems. What is not covered by our research is managing the demand. Managing demand may comprise a broad diversity of challenges, ranging from setting optimal prices to rationing the remaining capacity. Analyzing the impact of the demand process on profits and deriving optimal behavior for a given demand process will likely yield interesting opportunities for future research on rail car rental systems.

2.9 Proofs

Proof of Theorem 2.1. At first, we analyze the steady state distribution of the number of busy cars. Fakinos and Sirakoulis (1989) have shown that in a loss system equivalent to our rental system, the probability of having a set of n_j groups of size j ($j = 1..c$) in the system is of product-form. Their argument is based on the observation that a loss system with groups of different sizes j, c servers, and a homogeneous compound Poisson arrival stream with rate λ and order size mean q is equivalent to a parallel network of c single servers with a state-dependent arrival rate. Each server can serve one group at a time, regardless of its size. Assume that the number of customers in this network is $\sum_{j=1}^{c} jn_j = k$. Then, the arrival rate of a group of size j is $\lambda f(j)$ if $j < c - k$ and $\lambda (1 - F(j-1))$ if $j = c - k$. The state-dependent arrival rate of groups of size $j > c - k$ is 0. The steady state distribution of such a network is of product-form, if and only if the order size distribution is geometric or lattice geometric (cf. Fakinos and Sirakoulis (1989)). By rewriting Eq. (16) of Fakinos and Sirakoulis (1989), we get

$$p(n_1, ..., n_c) = B_c \psi(\sum_{j=1}^{c} jn_j) \left(\prod_{j=1}^{c} \frac{(\lambda f(j) \overline{S})^{n_j}}{n_j!} \right) \tag{2.18}$$

as the steady state distribution of state $(n_1, ..., n_c)$ (n_i denotes the number of groups of size i currently in the system). B_c denotes the normalizing constant, function $\psi(k)$ is defined as $\psi(k) = 1$ for $k = 0..c-1$, $\psi(c) = q$ and $\psi(k) = 0$ for all other k. Summing over all vector combinations such that $\sum_{j=1}^{c} jn_j = k$ gives (with the number of busy cars denoted by N)

$$\begin{aligned} P(N &= k \mid c\ cars) \\ &= B_c \psi(k) \sum_{\left\{(m_1,...,m_c) \mid \sum_{j=1}^{c} m_j = k\right\}} \prod_{j=1}^{c} \frac{(\lambda f(j) \overline{S})^{m_j/j}}{\left(\frac{m_j}{j}\right)!} \end{aligned} \tag{2.19}$$

with $m_j = jn_j$ and $n_j \in \mathbb{N}_0$. Define $(h_1 * h_2 * .. * h_c)(k)$ as the convolution of c functions

$$h_j(x) = \begin{cases} \frac{(\lambda f(j)\overline{S})^{x/j}}{\left(\frac{x}{j}\right)!} & \frac{j}{x} \in \mathbb{N}_0 \\ 0 & otherwise \end{cases}. \tag{2.20}$$

Then, by definition of the convolution operation, we get

$$\begin{aligned} P(N &= k \mid c\ cars) = B_c\psi(k)(h_1 * h_2 * .. * h_c)(k) \\ &= B_c\psi(k)(h_1 * h_2 * .. * h_c * h_{c+1} * ...)(k) \\ &= B_c e^{\lambda\overline{S}}\psi(k)\left(\widehat{h}_1 * \widehat{h}_2 * .. * \widehat{h}_c * \widehat{h}_{c+1} * ...\right)(k) \end{aligned} \tag{2.21}$$

with $\widehat{h}_j(x) = e^{-\lambda f(j)\overline{S}}h_j(x)$. The second line of Eq. (2.21) is based on $h_j(0) = 1$ for all $j > 0$, while the third line of Eq. (2.21) relies on $\sum_{j=1}^{\infty}\lambda f(j)\overline{S} = \lambda\overline{S}$. Since $\widehat{h}_j(x)$ equals the pdf of a lattice Poisson distribution ($\widehat{h}_j(x) = f_{Poi(\lambda f(j)\overline{S})}(jx)$), $\left(\widehat{h}_1 * \widehat{h}_2 * .. * \widehat{h}_c * \widehat{h}_{c+1} * ...\right)(k)$ is the pdf of a compound Poisson distribution with Poisson mean $\lambda\overline{S}$ and order size distribution $f(j)$. Thus, the steady state distribution of the number of busy cars, N, is given by

$$P(N = k \mid c\ cars) = B_c e^{\lambda\overline{S}}\psi(k)g(k) = \begin{cases} \frac{g(k)}{G(c)+(q-1)g(c)} & 0 \leq k < c \\ \frac{qg(c)}{G(c)+(q-1)g(c)} & k = c \\ 0 & k > c \end{cases} \tag{2.22}$$

with $g(k)$ as the pdf of a compound Poisson distribution and $G(k)$ its cdf. Then, the blocking probability $\beta(c)$ can be derived by using the well-known Law of Little and we obtain

$$\begin{aligned} L &= E(A)W \Rightarrow E(N|\ c\ cars) = \lambda q(1 - \beta(c))\overline{S} \\ &\Leftrightarrow \beta(c) = 1 - \frac{E(N|\ c\ cars)}{\lambda q\overline{S}} \\ &= 1 - \frac{\left(\sum\limits_{k=0}^{c} kg(k)\right) + c(q-1)g(c)}{\lambda q\overline{S}(G(c) + (q-1)g(c))}. \end{aligned} \tag{2.23}$$

Next, we can simplify the expression for $g(k)$ by using the probability generating function, $\widetilde{P}_f(z)$, of $f(k)$ to derive a closed-form expression for $f^{a*}(k)$:

$$\begin{aligned}
\widetilde{P}_f(z) &= \sum_{k=0}^{\infty} f(k) z^k = \frac{1}{q-1} \sum_{k=1}^{\infty} \left(\frac{q-1}{q} z\right)^k = \frac{1}{q-1}\left(\frac{1}{1-\frac{q-1}{q}z} - 1\right) \\
\Longrightarrow & \ \widetilde{P}_{f^{a*}}(z) = \widetilde{P}_f(z)^a \\
&= \left(\frac{z}{q-(q-1)\,z}\right)^a = \left(\frac{1}{q-(q-1)\,z}\right)^a z^a. \qquad (2.24)
\end{aligned}$$

The first term of $\widetilde{P}_{f^{a*}}(z)$ is the probability generating function of a negative binomial distribution with pdf $h(k) = \binom{a+k-1}{k}\left(\frac{1}{q}\right)^a\left(\frac{q-1}{q}\right)^k$ (see Feller (1971)) and z^a is the probability generating function of a distribution that has event a with probability 1. Therefore,

$$\begin{aligned}
f^{a*}(k) &= \sum_{j=0}^{\infty} h(j) 1(k-j=a) = h(k-a) \\
&= \frac{(k-1)!}{(a-1)!\,(k-a)!}\left(\frac{1}{q-1}\right)^a \left(\frac{q-1}{q}\right)^k, \ \forall k \geq a. \qquad (2.25)
\end{aligned}$$

Note that $g(0) = e^{-\lambda \overline{S}}$. ■

Proof of Theorem 2.2. We prove the theorem by using sample path arguments. With sample path arguments, the ordering of stochastic processes is shown for any given realization of random variables. If the processes are ordered for any realization, the processes are stochastically ordered.

Consider three rental systems with identical, arbitrary arrival processes $\mathbf{A} = \{(A_j, B_j)\}$ and c, $c+1$, and $c+2$ cars, respectively. The rental times are deterministic with a length of $\overline{S} > 0$ time units. Define the number of served requests, V_{ij}, of batch j and scenario $i = 1, 2, 3$ as

$$V_{ij} = \min(B_j, c+i-1-N_{ij}), \qquad (2.26)$$

where N_{ij} is the number of busy cars when batch j arrives (but before batch j is served). N_{ij} is given by

$$N_{ij} = \sum_{k=0}^{j-1} \mathbf{1}(A_j < A_k + \overline{S})V_{ik} \tag{2.27}$$

with $i = 1, 2, 3$. Our objective is to show that the additional number of served customers from adding cars is decreasing in the fleet size. Therefore, we will show that

$$\sum_{k=0}^{j} (V_{3k} - 2V_{2k} + V_{1k}) \leq 0 \tag{2.28}$$

for all $j \geq 0$. We prove this by induction over customer order j. We begin by analyzing the case for $j = 0$. The system is assumed to be empty before the first arrival, i.e., $N_{i0} = 0$ for $i = 1, 2, 3$. For this case, we look at three different cases:

Case 1. $B_0 < c + 1$. Then, it is easy to see that

$$V_{30} - 2V_{20} + V_{10} = B_0 - 2B_0 + B_0 = 0. \tag{2.29}$$

Case 2. $B_0 = c + 1$. Then, we have

$$V_{30} - 2V_{20} + V_{10} = c + 1 - 2c - 2 + c = -1. \tag{2.30}$$

Case 3. $B_0 > c + 1$. In this case, it holds that

$$V_{30} - 2V_{20} + V_{10} = c + 2 - 2c - 2 + c = 0. \tag{2.31}$$

So, in any case, it holds that $V_{30} - 2V_{20} + V_{10} \leq 0$, and the induction claim holds for $j = 0$. Next, we show that Ineq. (2.28) holds also for $j > 0$, given that the induction hypothesis is true for any step $i < j$. We distinguish between two mutually exclusive cases.

Case 1. $(N_{3j} - 2N_{2j} + N_{1j} > 0)$. In this case, N_{ij} can be seen as a function of i which is convex around $i = 2$. With the same argumentation, the function $c + i - 1 - N_{ij}$ is concave around $i = 2$, because negating N_{ij} gives a concave function and adding a linear term preserves the second order property. Then, we have

$$\begin{aligned} V_{3j} - 2V_{2j} + V_{1j} &= \min(B_j, c+2-N_{3j}) \\ &\quad -2\min(B_j, c+1-N_{2j}) + \min(B_j, c-N_{1j}) \\ &\leq 0, \end{aligned} \tag{2.32}$$

because the minimum operator preserves concavity.

Case 2. ($N_{3j} - 2N_{2j} + N_{1j} \leq 0$). In this case, we can rewrite Eq. (2.28) to

$$\begin{aligned} &\sum_{k=0}^{j} (V_{3k} - 2V_{2k} + V_{1k}) \\ = &\sum_{k=0}^{\max(i|A_i+\overline{S}\leq A_j)} (V_{3k} - 2V_{2k} + V_{1k}) \\ + &\sum_{\max(i|A_i+\overline{S}\leq A_j)+1}^{j-1} (V_{3k} - 2V_{2k} + V_{1k}) + (V_{3j} - 2V_{2j} + V_{1j}) \\ = &\sum_{k=0}^{\max(i|A_i+\overline{S}\leq A_j)} (V_{3k} - 2V_{2k} + V_{1k}) \\ &+ (N_{3j} - 2N_{2j} + N_{1j}) + (V_{3j} - 2V_{2j} + V_{1j}) . \end{aligned} \tag{2.33}$$

By making use of the induction hypothesis for any $i < j$, we get

$$\begin{aligned} &\sum_{k=0}^{j} (V_{3k} - 2V_{2k} + V_{1k}) \\ \leq\ &(N_{3j} - 2N_{2j} + N_{1j}) + (V_{3j} - 2V_{2j} + V_{1j}) \\ =\ &\min(B_j + N_{3j}, c+2) - 2\min(B_j + N_{2j}, c+1) + \min(B_j + N_{1j}, c) \\ \leq\ &0. \end{aligned} \tag{2.34}$$

The last inequality stems from the fact that, due to the definition of *Case 2*, the function N_{ij} and therefore also the function $B_j + N_{ij}$ is concave in i around $i = 2$. The minimum operator preserves concavity. Thus, $\sum_{k=0}^{j} (V_{3k} - 2V_{2k} + V_{1k}) \leq 0$

holds for any realization of $\mathbf{A}$ and for every $j \geq 0$, even if $j \to +\infty$. If the mean demand, λq, is finite, the following limits exist and are ordered as

$$\begin{aligned} & \beta(\lambda, \overline{S}, c+2, q) - 2\beta(\lambda, \overline{S}, c+1, q) + \beta(\lambda, \overline{S}, c, q) \\ = & -\lim_{t\to\infty} \left(\frac{\sum_{k=0}^{\infty} \mathbf{1}(A_k \leq t)\,(V_{3k} - 2V_{2k} + V_{1k})}{\sum_{k=0}^{\infty} \mathbf{1}(A_k \leq t) B_k} \right) \geq 0. \end{aligned} \quad (2.35)$$

We proved Ineq. (2.35) for the case of deterministic rental times. Due to the insensitivity of the rental system to the rental time distribution (see discussion following Theorem 2.1), Ineq. (2.35) holds for all rental time distributions that have a mean value of $\overline{S}$. ■

Proof of Theorem 2.3. As in the proof of Theorem 2.2, we prove the theorem by using sample path arguments. Consider two rental systems with arbitrary arrival processes $\mathbf{A}_1 = \{(A_{1j}, B_{1j})\}$ and $\mathbf{A}_2 = \{(A_{2j}, B_{2j})\}$, c_1 and c_2 cars, and deterministic service time $\overline{S} > 0$. Denote the combined arrival process by $\mathbf{A} = \mathbf{A}_1 \cup \mathbf{A}_2 = \{(A_j, B_{1j}, B_{2j})\}$. For technical reasons, assume that the arrival times are strictly ordered, i.e., $A_j < A_{j+1}$. In the scenario with separated fleets, the cars of the first fleet can only serve the B_{1j} requests, while the cars of the second fleet can only serve the B_{2j} requests. In the scenario with merged fleets, cars of both fleets can serve all B_{1j} and B_{2j} requests. The number of served requests, V_{ij}, of batch j and scenario $i = \mathbf{1}, \mathbf{2}, \mathbf{12}$ is defined as

$$\begin{aligned} V_{1j} &= \min(B_{1j}, c_1 - N_{1j}),\ V_{2j} = \min(B_{2j}, c_2 - N_{2j}) \\ \text{and } V_{12j} &= \min(B_{1j} + B_{2j}, c_1 + c_2 - N_{12j}) \end{aligned} \quad (2.36)$$

where N_{ij} is the number of busy cars when batch j arrives (but before batch j is served). N_{ij} is given by

$$N_{ij} = \sum_{k=0}^{j-1} \mathbf{1}(A_j < A_k + \overline{S}) V_{ik} \quad (2.37)$$

for $i = \mathbf{1}, \mathbf{2}, \mathbf{12}$. Our objective is to show that merging fleets leads to more served customers. We will show that

$$\sum_{k=0}^{j} (V_{12k} - V_{1k} - V_{2k}) \geq 0 \tag{2.38}$$

for all $j \geq 0$. We prove this by induction over customer order j. We begin by analyzing the case for $j = 0$. The system is assumed to be empty before the first arrival, i.e., $N_{i0} = 0$ for $i = \mathbf{1}, \mathbf{2}, \mathbf{12}$. By making use of the following relationship

$$\min(x_1 + x_2, y_1 + y_2) - \min(x_1, y_1) - \min(x_2, y_2) \geq 0, \tag{2.39}$$

it is easy to see that

$$V_{10} + V_{20} = \min(B_{10}, c_1) + \min(B_{20}, c_2) \leq \min(B_{10} + B_{20}, c_1 + c_2) = V_{120}. \tag{2.40}$$

For the induction step, assume that $\sum_{k=0}^{i} (V_{12k} - V_{1k} - V_{2k}) \geq 0$ holds for all $i < j$ (induction hypothesis). A direct consequence of this hypothesis is

$$\begin{aligned} N_{12j} - N_{1j} - N_{2j} &= \sum_{k=0}^{j-1} \mathbf{1}(A_j < A_k + \overline{S}) (V_{12k} - V_{1k} - V_{2k}) \\ &= \sum_{k=0}^{j-1} (V_{12k} - V_{1k} - V_{2k}) - \sum_{k=0}^{\max(i|A_i + \overline{S} \leq A_j)} (V_{12k} - V_{1k} - V_{2k}) \\ &\leq \sum_{k=0}^{j-1} (V_{12k} - V_{1k} - V_{2k}). \end{aligned} \tag{2.41}$$

Next, we show that Ineq. (2.38) holds for j if the induction hypothesis is true for any $i < j$. We analyze two mutually exclusive and collectively exhaustive cases:

Case 1. ($N_{1j} + N_{2j} - N_{12j} \geq 0$). This implies that

$$\begin{aligned} V_{12j} - V_{1j} - V_{2j} &= \min(B_{1j} + B_{2j}, c_1 + c_2 - N_{12j}) \\ &\quad - \min(B_{1j}, c_1 - N_{1j}) - \min(B_{2j}, c_2 - N_{2j}) \\ &\geq \min(B_{1j} + B_{2j}, c_1 + c_2 - N_{1j} - N_{2j}) \\ &\quad - \min(B_{1j}, c_1 - N_{1j}) - \min(B_{2j}, c_2 - N_{2j}) \\ &\geq 0 \end{aligned} \tag{2.42}$$

$$\begin{aligned} &\Rightarrow \sum_{k=0}^{j} (V_{12k} - V_{1k} - V_{2k}) \\ &= \sum_{k=0}^{j-1} (V_{12k} - V_{1k} - V_{2k}) + (V_{12j} - V_{1j} - V_{2j}) \geq 0. \end{aligned} \tag{2.43}$$

The inequality is based on Inequality (2.39).

Case 2. ($N_{1j} + N_{2j} - N_{12j} < 0$). This implies that

$$\begin{aligned} &V_{12j} - V_{1j} - V_{2j} \\ =\ &\min(B_{1j} + B_{2j}, c_1 + c_2 - N_{12j}) \\ &- \min(B_{1j}, c_1 - N_{1j}) - \min(B_{2j}, c_2 - N_{2j}) \\ =\ &\min(B_{1j} + B_{2j} + N_{12j}, c_1 + c_2) \\ &- \min(B_{1j} + N_{1j}, c_1) - \min(B_{2j} + N_{2j}, c_2) + N_{1j} + N_{2j} - N_{12j} \\ \geq\ &\min(B_{1j} + B_{2j} + N_{1j} + N_{2j}, c_1 + c_2) \\ &- \min(B_{1j} + N_{1j}, c_1) - \min(B_{2j} + N_{2j}, c_2) + N_{1j} + N_{2j} - N_{12j} \\ \geq\ &N_{1j} + N_{2j} - N_{12j}. \end{aligned} \tag{2.44}$$

The first inequality is based on Inequality (2.39). Then, by making use of Ineqs.

(2.41) and (2.44), we have

$$\begin{aligned}\sum_{k=0}^{j}(V_{12k}-V_{1k}-V_{2k}) &= \sum_{k=0}^{j-1}(V_{12k}-V_{1k}-V_{2k})+V_{12j}-V_{1j}-V_{2j}\\ &\geq N_{12j}-N_{1j}-N_{2j}+N_{1j}+N_{2j}-N_{12j}\\ &= 0. \qquad (2.45)\end{aligned}$$

Thus, $\sum_{k=0}^{j}(V_{12k}-V_{1k}-V_{2k})\geq 0$ holds for any realization of $\mathbf{A}$ and for every $j\geq 0$, even if $j\to+\infty$. If the mean demand, $(\lambda_1+\lambda_2)\,q$, is finite, the following limits exist and are ordered as

$$\begin{aligned}&L(\lambda_1+\lambda_2,\overline{S},c_1+c_2,q)-L(\lambda_1,\overline{S},c_1,q)-L(\lambda_2,\overline{S},c_2,q)\\ =&-\lim_{t\to\infty}\left(\frac{\sum_{k=0}^{\infty}\mathbf{1}(A_k\leq t)\,(V_{12k}-V_{1k}-V_{2k})}{t}\right)\leq 0. \qquad (2.46)\end{aligned}$$

As in the proof of Theorem 2.2, we proved Ineq. (2.46) for the case of deterministic rental times, which then holds for all rental time distributions that have a mean value of $\overline{S}$. Smith and Whitt (1981) showed a similar result for rental times that are i.i.d. for all customers. ■

Proof of Proposition 2.1.

The limit of ΔL with $\overline{S}_2\to+\infty$ is greater than zero, because of the following argumentation:

$$\begin{aligned}\lim_{\overline{S}_2\to\infty}\Delta L &= \lim_{\overline{S}_2\to\infty}L(\lambda_1+\lambda_2,\frac{\lambda_1\overline{S}_1+\lambda_2\overline{S}_2}{\lambda_1+\lambda_2},c_1+c_2,q)\\ &\quad -L(\lambda_1,\overline{S}_1,c_1,q)-\lim_{\overline{S}_2\to\infty}L(\lambda_2,\overline{S}_2,c_2,q)\\ &= (\lambda_1+\lambda_2)\,q-\lambda_2 q-L(\lambda_1,\overline{S}_1,c_1,q)\\ &> 0 \qquad (2.47)\end{aligned}$$

for $\overline{S}_1<+\infty$, $c_1>0$, and $\lambda>0$. Then, by the definition of the limit, there is a $\overline{S}_2'$ such that $\Delta L>0$ for every $\overline{S}_2>\overline{S}_2'$. ■

Proof of Proposition 2.2. At first, we will show that the optimal fleet size becomes $c_2^* = 0$ for large values of $\overline{S}_2$. Then, we show that $\Delta\Pi \leq 0$ for all $\overline{S}_2$ greater than some $\overline{S}_2'$. For c_2^* to be greater than zero, we must have $\Pi(\lambda_2, \overline{S}_2, 1, q) - \Pi(\lambda_2, \overline{S}_2, 0, q) > 0$. Hence, it must hold that

$$\begin{aligned}
& \Pi(\lambda_2, \overline{S}_2, 1, q) - \Pi(\lambda_2, \overline{S}_2, 0, q) \\
= \; & -(r_2 + p_2)\lambda_2 q \beta(\lambda_2 \overline{S}_2, 1, q) - h_2 \\
& +(r_2 + p_2)\lambda_2 q \beta(\lambda_2 \overline{S}_2, 0, q) \\
> \; & 0 \\
\Rightarrow \; & (r_2 + p_2)\lambda_2 q \left(1 - \beta(\lambda_2 \overline{S}_2, 1, q)\right) > h_2 \\
\Rightarrow \; & \lambda_2 q \left(1 - \beta(\lambda_2 \overline{S}_2, 1, q)\right) > \frac{h_2}{r_2 + p_2}. \qquad (2.48)
\end{aligned}$$

The term $\lambda_2 q \left(1 - \beta(\lambda_2 \overline{S}_2, 1, q)\right)$ is the mean contribution of the first car. However, this quantity is bounded above by $\frac{1}{\overline{S}_2}$ (Note that $\lambda_2 q \left(1 - \beta(\lambda_2 \overline{S}_2, 1, q)\right) = \frac{1}{\overline{S}_2}$ would be an optimal situation in which the car has no idle time). Hence, if

$$\frac{1}{\overline{S}_2} < \frac{h_2}{r_2 + p_2}, \qquad (2.49)$$

condition (2.48) cannot be met and the optimal fleet size is $c_2^* = 0$. Since $\overline{S}_2 \to +\infty$, Inequality (2.49) will hold for all $h_2 \overline{S}_2 > r_2 + p_2$. Then, we can see that the change in profit is less than zero if $\overline{S}_2 \to +\infty$:

$$\begin{aligned}
\lim_{\overline{S}_2 \to \infty} \Delta\Pi &= \lim_{\overline{S}_2 \to \infty} \Pi\left(\lambda_1 + \lambda_2, \frac{\lambda_1 \overline{S}_1 + \lambda_2 \overline{S}_2}{\lambda_1 + \lambda_2}, c_{12}^*(\overline{S}_2), q\right) \\
&\quad -\Pi(\lambda_1, \overline{S}_1, c_1^*, q) - \lim_{\overline{S}_2 \to \infty} \Pi(\lambda_2, \overline{S}_2, c_2^*(\overline{S}_2), q) \\
&= -p\left(\lambda_1 + \lambda_2\right) q + p\lambda_2 q - \Pi(\lambda_1, \overline{S}_1, c_1^*, q) \\
&= -p\lambda_1 q - \Pi(\lambda_1, \overline{S}_1, c_1^*, q) < 0 \qquad (2.50)
\end{aligned}$$

for $c_1^* > 0$, and $\lim_{\overline{S}_2 \to \infty} \Delta\Pi = 0$ for $c_1^* = 0$. The last inequality stems from the fact that $\Pi(\lambda_1, \overline{S}_1, 0, q) = -p\lambda_1 q$ and the optimality of c_1^*. Then, by the definition of the limit, there is a $\overline{S}_2'$ such that $\Delta\Pi < 0$ for every $\overline{S}_2 > \overline{S}_2'$ (with $c_1^* > 0$). ■

Proof of Proposition 2.3. We analyze the change in monetary lost sales, $\Delta L^{(m)}$, in the case of $\frac{r_1+p_1}{\overline{S}_1} = \frac{r_2+p_2}{\overline{S}_2}$. This change is less than or equal to zero, because

$$\begin{aligned}
\Delta L^{(m)} &= (r_{12}+p_{12})(\lambda_1+\lambda_2)\,q\beta(\lambda_1\overline{S}_1+\lambda_2\overline{S}_2, c_1+c_2, q) \\
&\quad -(r_1+p_1)\,\lambda_1 q\beta(\lambda_1\overline{S}_1, c_1, q)-(r_2+p_2)\,\lambda_2 q\beta(\lambda_2\overline{S}_2, c_2, q) \\
&= \frac{r_{12}+p_{12}}{\overline{S}_{12}}L(\lambda_1\overline{S}_1+\lambda_2\overline{S}_2, 1, c_1+c_2, q) \\
&\quad -\frac{r_1+p_1}{\overline{S}_1}L(\lambda_1\overline{S}_1, 1, c_1, q)-\frac{r_2+p_2}{\overline{S}_2}L(\lambda_2\overline{S}_2, 1, c_2, q) \\
&= \frac{r_1+p_1}{\overline{S}_1}\begin{pmatrix} L(\lambda_1\overline{S}_1+\lambda_2\overline{S}_2, 1, c_1+c_2, q) \\ -L(\lambda_1\overline{S}_1, 1, c_1, q)-L(\lambda_2\overline{S}_2, 1, c_2, q)\end{pmatrix} \\
&\leq 0
\end{aligned} \tag{2.51}$$

where $r_{12}+p_{12} = \frac{(r_1+p_1)\lambda_1+(r_2+p_2)\lambda_2}{\lambda_1+\lambda_2}$ and $\overline{S}_{12} = \frac{\overline{S}_1\lambda_1+\overline{S}_2\lambda_2}{\lambda_1+\lambda_2}$. The inequality is based on Theorem 2.3. ■

Example 2.1 *We give an example of two fleets with identical rental time distributions for which merging is not beneficial. Suppose we have two fleets with* $c_1 = c_2 = 2$ *cars. All orders of both fleets have i.i.d. rental times. Rental times are either* $\frac{2}{10}$ *or* $\frac{4}{10}$ *with a probability of 50% each. The arrival processes of both fleets repeat every time unit, e.g., every week and are given by Table 2.10. The parameter* ε *can have any value in the range* $0 < \varepsilon \leq \frac{1}{20}$*. It is easy to analyze*

No.	Fleet	Arrival Time	Batch Size
1	1	j	4
2	2	$j+\varepsilon$	1
3	2	$j+2\varepsilon$	1
4	2	$j+\frac{3}{10}$	1

Table 2.10: Arrivals at both fleets in time unit j (e.g. jth week)

the blocking probability before and after merging the two fleets. Since the arrival process repeats itself every time unit and since the system is empty at time instants $j = 0, 1, 2, \ldots$*, it suffices to calculate the blocking probabilities of the first time unit.*

Consider the case with separate fleets first:

$$\begin{aligned} L_1 &= 2 \qquad (2.52)\\ L_2 &= 1 \cdot P(N(t = \frac{3}{10}) = 2) \\ &= P(S > \frac{3}{10} - \varepsilon) P(S > \frac{3}{10} - 2\varepsilon) = \frac{1}{2} \cdot \frac{1}{2}. \qquad (2.53) \end{aligned}$$

In the case of merged fleets, the overall loss rate is

$$L_{12} = 2 + P(N(t = \frac{3}{10}) = 4) = 2 + P(S > \frac{3}{10}) = 2 + \frac{1}{2}. \qquad (2.54)$$

Then, we have

$$\Delta L = L_{12} - L_1 - L_2 = 2 + \frac{1}{2} - 2 - \frac{1}{4} > 0. \qquad (2.55)$$

The total loss rate increases with merging and, thus, fleet merging would reduce the overall profit.

Proof of Proposition 2.4. The profit share of time period t is

$$\Pi_t(c, l_t) = r\lambda_t q_t - (r + p)\, \lambda_t q_t \beta_t(c + l_t) - \frac{h}{T} c - v l_t, \qquad (2.56)$$

and the first difference function in $l_t \geq 0$ is

$$\begin{aligned} \Delta\Pi_t(c, l_t) &= \Pi_t(c, l_t + 1) - \Pi_t(c, l_t) \\ &= -(r + p)\, \lambda_t q_t \beta_t(c + l_t + 1) \\ &\quad -v\,(l_t + 1) + (r + p)\, \lambda_t q_t \beta_t(c + l_t) + v l_t \\ &= -(r + p)\, \lambda_t q_t \left[\Delta\beta_t(c + l_t)\right] - v. \qquad (2.57) \end{aligned}$$

Assume that $c \geq \widehat{l_t}^*$. Then, by definition of $\widehat{l_t}^*$, i.e.,

$$\widehat{l_t}^* = \min\left[\widehat{l} \mid \Delta\beta_t(\widehat{l}) \geq -\frac{v}{(r + p)\, \lambda_t q_t}\right], \qquad (2.58)$$

we obtain

$$\begin{aligned} 0 \quad &\geq \quad -(r+p)\,\lambda_t q_t \Delta\beta_t(c) - v \\ &\Longrightarrow \quad 0 \geq -(r+p)\,\lambda_t q_t \Delta\beta_t(c+l_t) - v \\ &\Longrightarrow \quad \Delta\Pi_t(c,l_t) \leq 0 \end{aligned} \tag{2.59}$$

for any $l_t \geq 0$, and it follows that leasing more cars reduces the expected profit. We get $l_t^*(c) = 0$ for $c \geq \widehat{l_t}^*$. Next, assume that $c < \widehat{l_t}^*$. Again, by definition of $\widehat{l_t}^*$, we have

$$\begin{aligned} -v \quad &> \quad (r+p)\,\lambda_t q_t \Delta\beta_t(c) \\ &\Longrightarrow \quad 0 < -(r+p)\,\lambda_t q_t \Delta\beta_t(c) - v \\ &\Longrightarrow \quad \Delta\Pi_t(c,0) > 0 \end{aligned} \tag{2.60}$$

and we can increase the expected profit by increasing l_t until the profit decreases for the first time. This point is, by definition, $l_t = \widehat{l_t}^* - c$. We obtain $l_t^*(c) = \left[\widehat{l_t}^* - c\right]^+$. ■

Proof of Proposition 2.5. The expected profit in time period t for optimal $l_t^*(c)$ is given by

$$\begin{aligned} \Pi_t(c, l_t^*(c)) \quad = \quad & r\lambda_t q_t \\ & -(r+p)\,\lambda_t q_t \beta_t(c + \left[\widehat{l_t}^* - c\right]^+) - \frac{h}{T}c - v\left[\widehat{l_t}^* - c\right]^+. \end{aligned} \tag{2.61}$$

The first difference function of $\Pi_t(c, l_t^*(c))$ in c is

$$\Delta\Pi_t(c, l_t^*(c)) = \begin{cases} -\frac{h}{T} + v, & \widehat{l_t}^* - c > 0, \\ -(r+p)\,\lambda_t q_t \Delta\beta_t(c) - \frac{h}{T}, & \widehat{l_t}^* - c \leq 0. \end{cases} \tag{2.62}$$

Since $-\frac{h}{T} + v$ is independent of c and by Theorem 2.2 $-(r+p)\,\lambda_t q_t \Delta\beta_t(c)$ is non-increasing in c, $\Pi_t(c, l_t^*(c))$ is concave in c. From $\widehat{\Pi}(c, \mathbf{l}^*(c)) = \sum_{t=1}^{T} \Pi_t(c, l_t^*(c))$ follows concavity of $\widehat{\Pi}(c, \mathbf{l}^*(c))$. ■

Proof of Proposition 2.6. Assume that the rental system has fleet size c^*, which is optimal if no leasing option exists. For each time period t, one of two cases applies.

Case 1: $\widehat{l}_t^* \leq c^*$. Then, $l_t^*(c^*) = \left[\widehat{l_t}^* - c^*\right]^+ = l_t^*(c^*+1) = \left[\widehat{l_t}^* - c^* - 1\right]^+ = 0$, i.e., the leasing option is neither used for c^* nor for c^*+1, and for any such time period

$$\Delta\Pi_t(c^*, l_t^*(c^*)) = \Delta\Pi_t(c^*, 0) = \Delta\Pi_t(c^*). \tag{2.63}$$

Case 2: $\widehat{l}_t^* > c^*$. Then, $l_t^*(c^*) = \left[\widehat{l}_t^* - c^*\right]^+ > 0$, i.e., the leasing option is actually used. By Eq. (2.62), we have

$$\begin{aligned} & \Delta\Pi_t(c^*, l_t^*(c^*)) - \Delta\Pi_t(c^*) \\ = \; & -\frac{h}{T} + v + (r+p)\,\lambda_t q_t \Delta\beta_t(c^*) + \frac{h}{T} \\ = \; & (r+p)\,\lambda_t q_t \Delta\beta_t(c^*) + v < 0, \end{aligned} \tag{2.64}$$

where the last inequality stems from

$$\begin{aligned} \widehat{l}_t^* \; &= \; \min\left[\widehat{l} \mid \Delta\beta_t(\widehat{l}) \geq -\frac{v}{(r+p)\,\lambda_t q_t}\right] \\ &\Longrightarrow \; (r+p)\,\lambda_t q_t \Delta\beta_t(c) + v < 0 \end{aligned} \tag{2.65}$$

for any $c < \widehat{l}_t^*$. From Eq. (2.63) and Ineq. (2.64) and the optimality of c^* in the case without leasing option, we have

$$\sum_{t=1}^{T} \Delta\Pi_t(c^*, l_t^*(c^*)) \leq \sum_{t=1}^{T} \Delta\Pi_t(c^*) \leq 0. \tag{2.66}$$

This proves that c_l^* with leasing option is less than or equal to c^* without leasing option, because $\widehat{\Pi}(c, \mathbf{l}^*(c))$ is concave in c and if $\Delta\widehat{\Pi}(c^*, \mathbf{l}^*(c^*)) \leq 0$, the optimizer c_l^* of this function must be less than or equal to c^*. ■

Proof of Proposition 2.7. The distribution of the number of busy cars in a loss system with infinitely many cars, N^∞, is given by $g(k)$ as defined in Theorem 2.1. We used this distribution to compute the blocking probability in Eq. (2.3).

We base our approximation of the blocking probability on an approximation of $g(k)$ by a normal distribution. We fit the normal distribution by equating means and variances of both distributions. The mean $E(N^\infty)$ is given by $E(N^\infty) = \lambda\overline{S}q$ and the variance $Var(N^\infty)$ is given by

$$Var(N^\infty) = \lambda\overline{S}Var(B) + \lambda\overline{S}E(B)^2 = \lambda\overline{S}q(q-1) + \lambda\overline{S}q^2 = \lambda\overline{S}q(2q-1). \quad (2.67)$$

Using a normal approximation is adequate, because for fixed q, $g(k)$ converges to a normal distribution if $\lambda\overline{S} \to +\infty$ (see Moehle (2005)). Next, we can simply replace $g(k)$ in Eq. (2.3) by a normal distribution:

$$\begin{aligned}\beta(c) \approx\ & 1 - \frac{\left(\sum_{k=0}^{c} k\left(\Phi(z(k+\frac{1}{2})) - \Phi(z(k-\frac{1}{2}))\right)\right)}{\lambda q\overline{S}\left(\Phi(z(c)) + (q-1)\left(\Phi(z(c+\frac{1}{2})) - \Phi(z(c-\frac{1}{2}))\right)\right)} \\ & - \frac{c(q-1)\left(\Phi(z(c+\frac{1}{2})) - \Phi(z(c-\frac{1}{2}))\right)}{\lambda q\overline{S}\left(\Phi(z(c)) + (q-1)\left(\Phi(z(c+\frac{1}{2})) - \Phi(z(c-\frac{1}{2}))\right)\right)}\end{aligned} \quad (2.68)$$

with $z(x) = \frac{x - E(N^\infty)}{\sqrt{Var(N^\infty)}}$. We can further simplify this result by replacing the sum in the numerator by a continuous approximation:

$$\begin{aligned}\beta(c) & \\ \approx\ & 1 - \frac{\int_{-\infty}^{c} x\phi(z(x))dx + c(q-1)\left(\Phi(z(c+\frac{1}{2})) - \Phi(z(c-\frac{1}{2}))\right)}{\lambda q\overline{S}\left(\Phi(z(c)) + (q-1)\left(\Phi(z(c+\frac{1}{2})) - \Phi(z(c-\frac{1}{2}))\right)\right)} \\ \approx\ & 1 - \frac{E(N^\infty)\Phi(z(c)) - \sqrt{Var(N^\infty)}\phi(z(c))}{E(N^\infty)\left(\Phi(z(c)) + (q-1)\left(\Phi(z(c+\frac{1}{2})) - \Phi(z(c-\frac{1}{2}))\right)\right)} \\ & - \frac{c(q-1)\left(\Phi(z(c+\frac{1}{2})) - \Phi(z(c-\frac{1}{2}))\right)}{E(N^\infty)\left(\Phi(z(c)) + (q-1)\left(\Phi(z(c+\frac{1}{2})) - \Phi(z(c-\frac{1}{2}))\right)\right)}.\end{aligned} \quad (2.69)$$

Note that in Eq. (2.69) we used the well-known relationship $\int_{c}^{+\infty} \frac{x-\mu}{\sigma}\phi\left(\frac{x-\mu}{\sigma}\right)dx = \phi\left(\frac{c-\mu}{\sigma}\right)$ of the normal distribution. ■

Chapter 3

Convexity of Loss Probabilities

3.1 Introduction

In this chapter, we discuss convexity of loss probabilities of a general class of stochastic loss models. Convexity of loss probabilities is identical to concavity of the service level of a stochastic system.

The structure of this chapter differs in some respects from the structure of chapters 2, 4, and 5. Because of its short length, introduction, literature review, and model description are grouped together in one section. The proofs are given in the analysis section, because they could not be separated from the corresponding analysis.

Let customer i arrive at time t_i, $0 \leq t_1 \leq t_2 \cdots$, at a c-server *loss system*, where arriving customers who find all servers busy leave without service and are lost. When well defined, let *loss probability* B_c be the (long run) fraction of customers lost. Number the servers $1, 2, \ldots,$ and suppose that each customer's service time does not depend on which server serves that customer. Without loss of generality, let each customer be served by the lowest-numbered server that is free.

For a fixed collection of arrival and service times, this way of assigning customers to servers allows us to consider simultaneously a series of loss systems as we vary $c \geq 1$. For any fixed c, customers not served by the first c servers *overflow* that loss

F. Papier, *Optimization of Rental Systems*, Edition KWV,
https://doi.org/10.1007/978-3-658-24313-5_3

system, and the arrival process of these customers, who are available to be served by the remaining servers, is called an *overflow process.* Each successive server c *thins* (removes some of the points from) the original arrival process.

It is immediate that B_c decreases as c increases. The quantity $B_c - B_{c+1}$ is the reduction in the loss probability achieved by going from c servers to $c+1$. Customers served by server $c+1$ account for this reduction. It has long been of great interest to know conditions under which this quantity also decreases as c increases, or equivalently, that the function $\{B_c\}$ is convex. When these probabilities are well defined, convexity is equivalent to this: In the long run, and for every c, server c serves more (at least as many) customers as server $c+1$.

Consider the problem of allocating a fixed total number of *interchangeable* (or *homogeneous*) servers to a set of loss systems, each with its own arrival process and service times. Finding the optimal allocation (that minimizes, say, the sum or a weighted sum of loss probabilities over the set) is much easier when the loss-probability function for each loss system is convex.

Until recently, the conditions under which $\{B_c\}$ was known to be convex were quite limited. Messerli (1972) showed that $\{B_c\}$ is *strictly* convex for the $M/G/c$ loss system. In 2002, Wolff and Wang showed that $\{B_c\}$ is convex but not necessarily strictly convex under conditions we call **AI**: Arbitrary arrivals and i.i.d. service times, independent of the arrival process.

Arbitrary arrivals includes the possibility that some customers arrive together in batches. Consider the situation where a batch of size b customers arrives to find only $i < b$ idle servers. What happens? Under *partial batch blocking* (PBB), i of these customers are served, and $b-i$ are lost. Under *entire batch blocking* (EBB), all b customers are lost. It is easy to think of circumstances where each of these possibilities is reasonable. For a party of b customers arriving at a restaurant, EBB; for our rail car rental systems, typically PBB.

The *thinning* of overflow processes, as discussed above, is valid under PBB, but not under EBB. As thinning plays a crucial role in the proof of convexity in Wolff and Wang (2002), PBB is implicitly assumed there.

But what about the result? We show by counterexample in Section 3.2 that under EBB and **AI**, $\{B_c\}$ is not necessarily convex.

In Section 3.2, we extend the convexity of $\{B_c\}$ to **Model 1**: The arrival process is arbitrary, and may have batches of customers with arbitrary batch sizes. Service times all have the same distribution, are independent of the arrival process and from batch to batch, but may be dependent within the same batch. When the circumstances arise, we have PBB.

Under batch Poisson arrivals and **Model 1**, specialized to *equal* service times within the same batch, a reasonable assumption in the examples above, several articles have studied conditions under which the blocking probabilities are insensitive to the service distribution, e.g., see Economou and Fakinos (1999). For i.i.d. service times within the same batch, however, insensitivity does not hold.

For convenience, we assume that service times and batch inter-arrival times are strictly positive. These assumptions remove ambiguity, such as about how the system deals with batches that arrive together, but are not strictly necessary.

We consider an arbitrary sample path of batch arrival times and batch sizes at server 1, where for arrival time t_i of batch i, $t_i \to \infty$ as $i \to \infty$. Each overflow process consists of the same batches, where each successive server thins the arrival process by removing one customer from some batches. Thus some batches may be empty, but we will ignore them, and assume that an infinite number of batches are not. Each overflow process retains the property that service times are i.i.d. from batch to batch, but may be dependent within the same batch.

As each server serves at most one customer from a batch, the service times of served customers at each server also are i.i.d.

Finally, we extend convexity in a different direction to what we call **Model 2**: The arrival process is arbitrary. Each server has a fixed number, $1, 2, \ldots$, where each customer is served at the lowest-numbered server that is free; this is called *ordered entry*. (Temporarily, suppose all batches are of size one.) The service time of every customer served at each server c is a random draw from some service distribution G_c, independent of all else at the time of the draw. This distribution *may depend on the server*, and servers are said to be *heterogeneous.*

Even though servers are no longer interchangeable, we define overflow processes as before, where each successive server thins the original arrival process. The service times of served customers at each server c are i.i.d. with distribution G_c.

For **Model 2** with renewal arrivals, exponential service, and service rate μ_c at server c that is *decreasing* (non-increasing) in c, Yao (1986) showed that $\{B_c\}$ is strictly convex. For another proof under the same assumptions, see p. 135 of Liyanage and Shanthikumar (1992).

In Section 3.3, we extend this result to **Model 2**, where instead of decreasing $\{\mu_c\}$, we assume this natural generalization: Distributions $G_1, G_2, \ldots$ are stochastically increasing (non-decreasing). To avoid complicating the argument, we initially assume that all batches are of size 1, and then relax this assumption. At the end of Section 3.3, we present an easy example showing that when $\{G_c\}$ is not stochastically increasing, convexity may fail.

For interchangeable servers, imposing an entry order is a convenience in the analysis. In some systems, such as conveyors, the physical layout of the servers determines the entry order. When servers are heterogeneous, this raises interesting design questions. With k servers, there are $k!$ ways to order them. They are not equivalent; in particular, B_k depends on the ordering. By this measure, the *optimal* order is the one that minimizes B_k.

Yao (1987) considered this issue and related more general ones, and showed that under renewal arrivals and exponential service, the optimal ordering is decreasing $\{\mu_c\}$, the same ordering assumed in Yao (1986). He also established a partial order for the $k!$ orderings, which showed, among other things, that increasing $\{\mu_c\}$ maximizes B_k. Shanthikumar and Yao (1987) extended these results to arbitrary arrival processes, and other extensions as well, but only for exponential service.

We discuss briefly the optimal-ordering problem in Section 3.3, where we show by counterexample (unfortunately) that for an arbitrary arrival process and general service distributions that can be stochastically ordered, stochastically increasing $\{G_c\}$ is not necessarily optimal.

In Section 3.4, we conclude our research.

3.2 Analysis of the Model With Homogeneous Servers

We assume **Model 1**. Consider servers c and $c+1$ and the overflow process at server c, where both servers are idle initially. This overflow process and the corresponding service times generate the thinned overflow process at server $c+1$ and the following:

Let X_n and Y_n be, respectively, the times of the nth service completion at servers c and $c+1$; $n \geq 1$. Let $J(t)$ and $K(t)$ be, respectively, the number of service completions by time t at servers c and $c+1$; $t \geq 0$.

For arbitrary fixed c, stochastic processes $\{X_n\}$ and $\{J(t)\}$ are determined entirely by the overflow process and the sequence of service times of served customers at server c. Not only are these service times i.i.d., they are also independent of the overflow process in this sense: Suppose a batch arrives at time t to find server c idle. The service time of each customer served at server c is a random draw from the service distribution, independent of the overflow process up to time t. We call these independence properties **IP**. It is possible that at the same time, customers with the same service distribution will begin service at servers such as $c-1$ and $c+1$. **IP** holds, regardless of the occurrence of such events. Note that while not stated explicitly, **IP** is required in Wolff and Wang (2002).

In addition to independent and equal service times within the same batch, dependence within batches may take many other forms that satisfy our **IP** assumption. To illustrate, for a batch of size 2, service distribution G, and random variable U that is uniformly distributed on $(0,1)$ and independent of all else, generate the two service times as $G^{-1}(U)$ and $G^{-1}(1-U)$.

Note that the sequences of i.i.d. service times of served customers at c and $c+1$

are *not* independent, as each server may serve, from time to time, a customer from the same batch. These sequences are independent in Wolff and Wang (2002).

We now introduce a new sequence of i.i.d. service times $\{S_n\}$ with the same distribution, *independent of all else*, and fix the arrival process at server 1 (arrival times and batch sizes). The sample space is the product space generated by the service times corresponding to the arrival process and this new sequence.

Now fix a point in the sample space. This determines the overflow processes at every server, where they are successively thinned. This also determines the service times of served customers at every server, and the stochastic processes introduced above.

For servers c and $c+1$, with the same fixed overflow process at each, we replace the sequence of service times of served customers by $\{S_n\}$. That is, we let S_n be the service time of the nth customer served at server c and also at server $c+1$.

These overflow processes and $\{S_n\}$ generate X'_n, corresponding to X_n, $J'(t)$, corresponding to $J(t)$, and so on. It is easy to check that when using $\{S_n\}$ in this manner, **IP** holds at both servers c and $c+1$. Hence each primed stochastic process is *stochastically equivalent* to the corresponding process without the prime,

$$\{X'_n\} \sim \{X_n\}, \{Y'_n\} \sim \{Y_n\}, \{J'(t)\} \sim \{J(t)\}, \text{ and } \{K'(t)\} \sim \{K(t)\}. \quad (3.1)$$

It is important to remember that stochastically equivalent processes have the same marginal and joint distributions, and limiting behavior.

We now couple primed processes at servers c and $c+1$.

As $X'_1 = t_1 + S_1$ and $Y'_1 \geq t_1 + S_1$, $X'_1 \leq Y'_1$. Now suppose that $X'_n \leq Y'_n$. As the first arrival after X'_n in the overflow process at server c occurs no later than the first arrival after Y'_n in the thinned process, $X'_{n+1} \leq Y'_{n+1}$. We have, for every point in the sample space,

$$X'_n \leq Y'_n, \text{ for } n = 1, 2, \ldots. \quad (3.2)$$

From (3.2), it follows immediately that for every point in the sample space,

$$J'(t) \geq K'(t), \text{ for all } t \geq 0. \tag{3.3}$$

From (3.3) and (3.1), and that the limits below exist,

$$\lim_{t\to\infty} J(t)/t = \lim_{t\to\infty} J'(t)/t \geq \lim_{t\to\infty} K'(t)/t = \lim_{t\to\infty} K(t)/t, \tag{3.4}$$

which implies the following result.

Theorem 3.1 *For a loss system under the assumptions in Model 1, $\{B_c\}$ is decreasing and convex.*

Under EBB, conditions for the convexity of $\{B_c\}$ are unknown, but would appear to be much more stringent. For example, if all batches are of size 3, and we have equal service times within each batch, $B_1 = B_2 = 1 > B_3 = B_4 = B_5$. By specializing to constant service, this example also shows that under EBB and **AI**, $\{B_c\}$ is not necessarily convex.

3.3 Analysis of the Model With Heterogeneous Servers and Ordered-Entry

We assume **Model 2**. As in Section 3.2, we compare service completions at servers c and $c+1$, and use the same notation for stochastic processes $\{X_n\}$, $\{Y_n\}$, $\{J(t)\}$, and$\{K(t)\}$. Assume $\{G_c\}$ is stochastically increasing and (initially) that all batches are of size 1.

Under the assumptions in **Model 2**, the service times of served customers at each server c are i.i.d., with distribution G_c. Furthermore, they have property **IP** at every server, as defined in Section 3.2.

Now let $\{U_n\}$ be an i.i.d. sequence of random variables, independent of all else, that are uniformly distributed on $(0, 1)$, and fix the arrival process at server 1. The sample space is the product space of the service times of the arrivals at server

1 and $\{U_n\}$.

Now fix a point in the sample space. This determines the overflow processes, the service times of served customers at every server, and the stochastic processes above.

For servers c and $c+1$, with the same fixed overflow process at each, we replace the sequence of service times of served customers by $\{S_n^c\}$ and$\{S_n^{c+1}\}$, respectively, where for every n, $S_n^c = G_c^{-1}(U_n)$ and $S_n^{c+1} = G_{c+1}^{-1}(U_n)$.

Now use these overflow processes and service time sequences to generate the four primed stochastic processes introduced in Section 3.2. Clearly, **IP** holds at both servers, and the stochastic equivalences in (3.1) remain valid.

The assumption that $\{G_c\}$ is stochastically increasing implies that at every sample point

$$S_n^c \leq S_n^{c+1}, n = 1, 2, \ldots. \tag{3.5}$$

Now begin the induction argument in Section 3.2 with: As $X_1' = t_1 + S_1^c$ and $Y_1' \geq t_1 + S_1^{c+1}$, $X_1' \leq Y_1'$, where we use (3.5). The rest of the induction argument goes through with these minor modifications and we have this result.

Theorem 3.2 *For a loss system under the assumptions in Model 2, where the* $\{G_c\}$ *are stochastically increasing,* $\{B_c\}$ *is decreasing and convex.*

Now suppose that some batches are of size > 1, assuming of course PBB. Independent service times within the same batch could be interpreted as independent service requirements, with service time distributions dependent on where each customer happens to get served. For example, some servers may be faster than others.

Dependent service times would mean dependent service requirements. If we were to simulate the operation of **Model 2**, we would use the same uniform random variable U to generate the service times of all customers in the same batch, combined with the appropriate G_c.

Either way, the primed processes would be generated in the same manner and convexity still holds.

When $\{G_c\}$ increases stochastically in **Model 2**, servers get progressively slower. Once we know that $\{B_c\}$ is convex for interchangeable servers, it should come as no surprise that this is true when servers get slower. Perhaps the easiest and certainly the most familiar example where convexity fails is this: Two servers with Poisson arrivals and exponential service at rate μ_i, $i = 1, 2$, where $\mu_2 >> \lambda > \mu_1$. Fix λ and μ_1, and let $\mu_2 \to \infty$. We have $B_1 = \lambda/(\lambda + \mu_1) > 1/2$ and $B_2 \to 0$.

The design questions raised at the end of Section 3.1 are important. Cooper and Palakurthi (1989) considered a two-server loss system with Poisson arrivals and service distributions G_a and G_b, where G_a is 2-Erlang and G_b is exponential. They showed that when G_a and G_b have the same mean, and hence even when G_a has a (slightly) larger mean, B_2 is smaller for ordering (G_a, G_b) than for (G_b, G_a). Hence ordering the service distributions from smallest to largest *mean* is not necessarily optimal. However, G_a and G_b are not stochastically ordered.

Now consider this simple example. We have a two-server loss system with deterministic service where G_a has mean 4 and G_b has mean 3. The system is empty initially, and suppose arrivals occur at $0, 1, 4.1, 4.2, 10, 11, 14.1, 14.2, \ldots$. We have $B_2 = 0$ for ordering (G_a, G_b), and $B_2 = 1/4$ for ordering (G_b, G_a). Thus arranging the servers in stochastically increasing service-time distributions, when possible, is not necessarily optimal under the general conditions of **Model 2**.

3.4 Conclusion

In this research, we considered stochastic loss models in which customers arrive and require service from a certain number of servers. Service times were assumed to be identically distributed with an arbitrary distribution. In our models, we assumed independence of the service times between batches, but allowed for dependent service times within batches. We showed that the loss probabilities of such models are convex in the number of servers if PBB is assumed. And we demonstrated by counterexample that convexity does not hold in general under EBB. At first, we analyzed the case of homogeneous servers. Afterwards, we extended the results to the case of heterogeneous servers which are ordered by stochastically decreasing service speed. Finally, we showed by counterexample that such an ordering does not, in contrast to models with exponential service times, lead to minimal loss probabilities. Appropriate conditions for optimality when the service times are not (all) exponential remains an interesting open problem.

Remark The results of this chapter have been published in Papier et al. (2007).

Chapter 4

Capacity Rationing and Fleet Sizing under Batch Arrivals

4.1 Introduction

Historically, cargo logistics companies have not differentiated between customers and have treated all orders equally. With increasing demand for high service quality on the one hand and increasing pressure to cut costs on the other hand, this is about to change. Some customers require high availability, e.g. when their production schedule depends on timely transportation. They are willing to pay a high price for the rental services in return for a guarantee that their order is served. Other customers are less dependent on availability but require service at low cost. Cargo logistics companies are beginning to leverage this difference in customer needs to improve profit.

In this chapter, we analyze a rental system that operates in such a situation. Our research has been motivated by a leading European rail cargo company that recently introduced service differentiation by offering two types of rental services: Premium service and classic service. Under premium service, customer pay more on the rental service than under classic service but receive a compensation when their demand is not filled. Under classic service, customers do not receive such a compensation. Both services are served by the same fleet of cargo rail cars, so that

F. Papier, *Optimization of Rental Systems*, Edition KWV,
https://doi.org/10.1007/978-3-658-24313-5_4

joint planning is necessary. In strategic planning, the company has to decide on the size of its rental fleet. In operational planning, it must decide how to allocate rail cars to customers.

We model the rental business as a queuing loss system with batch arrivals and explicitly take into account service differentiation. We maximize expected profit by optimizing the fleet size and the admission policy. The contribution of our research is threefold: Firstly, we extend existing rental models to batch arrivals which better capture the demand process in B2B settings such as the one that motivated our research. Secondly, we develop an algorithm to find the joint optimum of the fleet size and the admission policy. Thirdly, we analyze extensively the impact of system parameters such as order sizes, penalty cost or holding cost on the expected profit.

The remainder of this chapter is structured as follows: In Section 4.2, we review the relevant literature. In Section 4.3, we define the model, derive the objective function, and discuss the main assumptions of the model. In Section 4.4, we calculate the expected profit and optimize the decision variables. In Section 4.5, we perform numerical experiments which are based on fleet data from the company that motivated our research. From the experimental results, we derive implications for the management of rental businesses. In Section 4.6, we conclude. Section 4.7 contains the proofs.

4.2 Literature Review

In this chapter, we build on previous research on capacity rationing in stochastic queuing and rental systems. As to our best knowledge, Miller (1969) was the first to analyze rationing in loss systems. He studies a queuing loss system with multiple customer classes, single arrivals, and identical service time distributions for all customers and proves the optimality of threshold policies. Shonick and Jackson (1973) extend the model of Miller to a model in which one class of customers waits in a queue and the other one is blocked if the remaining capacity is low. They apply their model to capacity management of hospital beds. Lippman (1975) analyzes queuing loss models with a finite decision horizon. Albright (1977) studies queuing loss models with multiple customer classes in which some servers are faster than the others. Carrizosa et al. (1998) analyze a queuing loss system with multiple customer classes and arbitrary service time distributions in which a quota-based admission policy is used. The authors derive the optimal admission quotas for each class. Ku and Jordan (1997) and Ku and Jordan (2002) analyze admission control in queuing loss systems in which servers are connected sequentially and customers may require several processing steps.

All of the previously described research assumes single arrivals, but admission control has also been extended to batch arrivals. Kawanishi et al. (2000) study a queuing system with two customer classes and batched demand, in which one class of customers is blocked and the other one waits in a queue. Ross and Tsang (1989) and Altman et al. (2001) also study queuing loss models with batch arrivals. They allow for multiple customers classes and assume entire batch blocking. For the model with two customer classes, Altman et al. prove that a threshold policy is optimal. Örmeci and Burnetas (2004) analyze a queuing loss system with batch arrivals and multiple customer classes but with partial batch blocking. All customers are assumed to have the same service time distribution. They show the optimality of a threshold policy with threshold levels that are monotone in the class-specific revenues. Örmeci and Burnetas (2005) extend this model to class-specific service-time distributions. They conjecture but do not analytically prove the optimality of threshold policies.

Apart from the extension to batch arrivals, other extensions have recently been published. Örmeci and Van Der Wal (2006) consider single-arrival loss models with general interarrival times. For such models, the optimality of threshold policies could be shown. Ku et al. (2006) extend admission control to loss networks where customers are routed to other servers after they have received service at one server. Gans and Savin (2007) study a queuing loss model for rental businesses with two customer classes: contract customers and walk-in customers. Contract customers have fixed prices while walk-in customers are offered an individual price upon their arrival. The authors derive an optimal admission policy for contract customers and optimal prices for walk-in customers.

The idea of rationing has also been analyzed extensively in the context of inventory management. In inventory management, two or more customer classes request items from a common inventory. As with rental systems, rationing can be used to protect high-priority customers. While the idea of rationing in inventory management is identical to the idea of rationing in our research, the underlying methods differ considerably. For an overview on existing research in this context, we refer the interested reader to Zhao et al. (2005) or Tempelmeier (2006).

In this research, we analyze a stochastic rental system with two customer classes and compound Poisson distributed demand. Unlike previous research which focussed on analysis rather than on optimization, we show how to derive the optimal solution. We also study the effect of the system parameters on performance and derive managerial insights from this study. The objective function, the decision variables, and the model assumptions are described in detail in the next section.

4.3 Model Description

We consider a rental company that rents vehicles such as rail cars to commercial customers. The company operates a fleet of c homogeneous vehicles. The company offers two different services to its customers: *premium service (class 1)* and *classic service (class 2)*. The contribution margins are r_1 and r_2, respectively, with $r_1 \geq r_2$.

Customers arrive at random arrival times and demand a certain number of cars (this number is referred to as order size B_j). We assume that customer demands arrive according to two independent compound Poisson arrival streams. The arrival rate of class i orders is denoted by λ_i. The order size distribution of an order of class i is given by the probability mass function $f_i(n)$ with mean q_i and $F_i(0) = 0$. Order sizes can have an arbitrary distribution.

When a customer arrives, the rental company can decide whether to allocate the customer all requested cars, some cars or no cars at all. The admission decision of the jth customer is denoted by a_j. $a_j = n$ corresponds to an allocation of n cars, while $a_j = 0$ corresponds to a rejection. Obviously, the number of cars allocated must be less than or equal to the number of requested cars (B_j) and the number of idle cars upon arrival ($c - N_j^-$), $a_j \leq \min\left(B_j, c - N_j^-\right)$. Customers that are denied service are lost. Lost class 1 demand receives a compensation p per lost car. We denote a policy which specifies a_j for each arrival j by Γ.

Once customers are allocated cars, they hold them for a random period of time. The duration of a rental service is referred to as the *rental time*. We denote the mean of the rental time by $\overline{S} = \mu^{-1}$. It comprises delivery of the empty cars to the customer, loading operations, delivery of the cars to the destination, unloading operations, and the return to the rental company. After the customer has used a car, she returns it to the rail car company. Rental times are assumed to be i.i.d. random variables with an exponential distribution. This assumption is made by many articles on capacity rationing in rental systems (e.g. cf. Gans and Savin (2007), Kawanishi et al. (2000), or Örmeci and Burnetas (2004)), because class-specific rental time means or other rental time distributions limit the analytical tractability of the model and because this assumption reflects the idea that all rail cars are used in common processes, independent of the class origin.

On a long-term basis, the rental company can decide on the fleet size. On a short-term basis, it can decide on the admission policy. Thus, the decision variables are the fleet size c and the admission policy Γ. The objective of the rental company is to maximize expected profit per time unit. Profit consists of regular revenues and operating costs, penalties paid to customers, and holding costs for the fleet. The fleet size c and the admission policy Γ determine the expected amount of served class i demand per time unit, denoted by $V_i(c, \Gamma)$. The expected revenues are $r_1 V_1(c, \Gamma)$ for class 1 demand and $r_2 V_2(c, \Gamma)$ for class 2 demand. The rental company must pay a compensation for each unmet class 1 demand, which amounts, on average, to $p(\lambda_1 q_1 - V_1(c,\Gamma))$. Holding costs h arise per car and time unit, such that the whole fleet accrues holding costs of hc. The company's expected profit is then given by

$$\Pi(c,\Gamma) = r_1 V_1(c,\Gamma) + r_2 V_2(c,\Gamma) - p(\lambda_1 q_1 - V_1(c,\Gamma)) - hc. \tag{4.1}$$

4.4 Model Optimization

In this section, we optimize the model. Firstly, we characterize the optimal policy and demonstrate that it has a static rationing level. Secondly, we derive a closed-form expression for the expected profit given a certain fleet size and a rationing policy. Thirdly, we formulate an upper bound on the optimal fleet size which reduces the solution space to a finite set. This enables the use of standard optimization procedures to find the optimal fleet size and rationing level. Fourthly, we provide a counterexample to the intuitive idea that rationing always reduces the optimal fleet size.

Characterization of Optimal Policy We next show that the optimal admission policy is a threshold (rationing) policy. Due to the assumptions that interarrival times and service times are exponentially distributed and that service times are i.i.d., the system state is fully described by the total number of cars rented out, N. An admission decision is optimal, if the immediate reward r_j is greater than the expected loss from having one car less available, $E(L_j \mid N)$. It can easily be seen that if $E(L_j \mid N)$ is increasing in N, then there exists some threshold T_i for class i customers such that we would reject the customer for any system state $N \geq T_i$. We would intuitively expect that with more cars rented out, the danger of losing other customers is greater than with fewer cars rented out, i.e., $E(L_j \mid N)$ is increasing in N. A technical proof that this result indeed holds for a related admission control problem with positive rewards can be found in Örmeci and Burnetas (2004). Since we can transform our rental system into a system with positive rewards by rewriting the profit function (Equation (4.1)) to

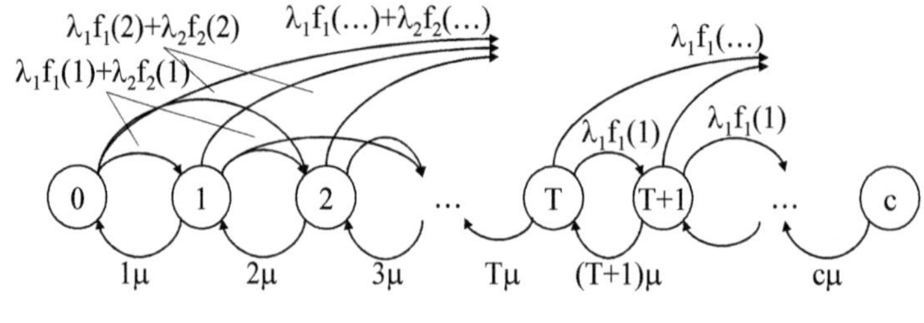

Figure 4.1: State transition diagram of the CTMC that describes the rental system

$\Pi(c,\Gamma) = (r_1 + p)\, V_1(c,\Gamma) + r_2 V_2(c,\Gamma) - p\lambda_1 q_1 - hc$ and since $-p\lambda_1 q_1 - hc$ is independent of the admission policy, we conclude that their result also applies to our rental system. We can see that $T_1 = c$, i.e. that as many high-priority customers as possible should be admitted. The reasoning is as follows: Assume the contrary that $T_1 < c$, then we could have the same admission policy with $c - T_1$ fewer cars and could set the $c - T_1$ cars aside to separately serve more customers. This policy cannot be optimal. The preceding ideas lead to the following corollary about the optimal admission policy.

Corollary 4.1 *The optimal admission policy Γ^* for a given fleet size is a threshold policy with constant threshold level $T^*(c)$. Thus, the optimal admission decision a_j^* is given by*

$$a_j^*(N_j = n, B_j = b) = \begin{cases} \min(c-n, b) & jth\ arrival\ is\ class\ 1 \\ \min([T-n]^+, b) & jth\ arrival\ is\ class\ 2. \end{cases} \tag{4.2}$$

Computation of Expected Profit Next, we analyze the expected performance of the rental model. The system state behaves according to a continuous-time, discrete-state Markov Chain (CTMC). Because the system state is N, the Markov Chain is one-dimensional. The state transition diagram of the corresponding CTMC is shown in Figure 4.1. Because the Markov Chain is irreducible and because it has a finite state space, it has a unique steady state solution (cf. Wolff (1989)), and its distribution $P(N = n)$ can be obtained by equating the inflow and the outflow of each state $n \geq 0$ (cf. Wolff (1989), p. 210). We get

$$
\begin{aligned}
&(n+1)\mu P(N=n+1)\\
&+\sum_{k=0}^{n-1}\left(\lambda_1 f_1(n-k)+\mathbf{1}(n=c)\lambda_1\overline{F}_1(c-k)\right)P(N=k)\\
&+\sum_{k=0}^{n-1}\left(\mathbf{1}(n\leq T)\lambda_2 f_2(n-k)+\mathbf{1}(n=T)\lambda_2\overline{F}_2(T-k)\right)P(N=k)\\
&=P(N=n)\left(n\mu+\lambda_1\mathbf{1}(n<c)+\lambda_2\mathbf{1}(n<T)\right)
\end{aligned}
\tag{4.3}
$$

for $n = 0...c-1$ (define $\sum_{n=0}^{-1} x_n = 0$). Note that all probabilities must sum up to 1, i.e., $\sum_{n=0}^{c} P(N = n) = 1$. After some algebraic manipulations of Equation (4.3), we obtain the following recursive steady state equation

$$
\begin{aligned}
P(N=n) &= \frac{1}{n\mu}P(N=n-1)\left((n-1)\,\mu+\lambda_1\mathbf{1}(n\leq c)+\lambda_2\mathbf{1}(n\leq T)\right)\\
&-\frac{1}{n\mu}\sum_{k=0}^{n-2}\lambda_1 f_1(n-1-k)P(N=k)\\
&-\frac{1}{n\mu}\sum_{k=0}^{n-2}\mathbf{1}(n\leq T+1)\lambda_2 f_2(n-1-k)P(N=k)\\
&-\frac{1}{n\mu}\sum_{k=0}^{n-2}\mathbf{1}(n=T+1)\lambda_2\overline{F}_2(T-k)P(N=k)
\end{aligned}
\tag{4.4}
$$

for $n = 1...c$.

From Equation (4.4), we can see that there are only additive recursive terms so that $P(N = n)$ can be expressed as $P(N = n) = w_n P(N = 0)$. This enables us to compute the steady state probabilities by the following algorithm:

Algorithm 4.1 *Computation of steady state probabilities*

1. *Set* $\widetilde{P}(N = 0) = 1$ *(or any other value).*
2. *Compute all* $\widetilde{P}(N = n)$ *for* $0 < n \leq c$ *with Equation (4.4).*

3. *Calculate* $w = \sum_{n=0}^{c} \widetilde{P}(N = n)$.
4. *Get* $P(N = n)$ *from* $P(N = n) = \frac{\widetilde{P}(N=n)}{w}$.

From the steady state distribution, the expected number of served customers of each class, V_1 and V_2, can be derived by taking expectations. This result is formally shown in the following proposition.

Proposition 4.1 *The expected number of served customers of each class,* V_1 *and* V_2*, are given by*

$$V_1(c,T) = \lambda_1 \sum_{n=0}^{c} P(N = n) \left(\sum_{b=0}^{c-n} b f_1(b) + (c-n)\overline{F}_1(c-n) \right) \tag{4.5}$$

and

$$V_2(c,T) = \lambda_2 \sum_{n=0}^{c} P(N = n) \left(\sum_{b=0}^{[T-n]^+} b f_2(b) + [T-n]^+ \overline{F}_2(T-n) \right). \tag{4.6}$$

The proof of this proposition is contained in Section 4.7. The profit $\Pi(c,T)$ under fleet size c and a threshold policy with parameter T follows from Equation (4.1).

Derivation of Upper Bound Next, we need to find the optimal parameter constellation (c^*, T^*) that maximizes $\Pi(c,T)$. Parameters c and T are defined on $0, 1, 2, ..$, so that we cannot simply enumerate the solution space to find the optimal values. We need additional properties of the profit function. Therefore, we derive an upper bound c_{ub} on the optimal fleet size c. Parameters c and T are discrete and using the upper bound, we can see that $0 \leq T \leq c \leq c_{ub}$ and the optimal solution can be found by numerical evaluation. The upper bound is given in the following proposition.

Proposition 4.2 *The optimal fleet size* c^* *cannot be greater than upper bound* c_{ub}*, i.e.,*

$$c^* \leq c_{ub} = \frac{(r_1 + p)\,\lambda_1 q_1 + r_2 \lambda_2 q_2}{h} \tag{4.7}$$

The proof of this proposition is contained in Section 4.7.

Counterexample to Intuitive Order of Optimal Fleet Sizes One might intuitively expect that the optimal fleet size without rationing c^*_{NoRat} is always greater than or equal to the optimal fleet c^* with optimal threshold level $T^*(c)$, because the rationing policy makes better use of the available cars. We see in the next section that this is indeed the case for most of the settings we analyzed. However, the following counterexample demonstrates that this idea does not hold in general.

Example 4.1 *We show that the optimal fleet size with rationing c^* can be greater than the optimal fleet size without rationing c^*_{NoRat}. Consider a rental system with parameters $\lambda_1 = 1$, $\lambda_2 = 4$, geometric order size distribution with $q_1 = q_2 = 10$, $\overline{S} = 1$, $r_1 = 2$, $r_2 = 1$, $p = 1$, and $h = 1.15$. For the case with rationing, $c^* = 7$ and $T^*(7) = 0$, i.e., all class 2 demand is blocked. Without rationing, $c^*_{NoRat} = 3$, so that $c^* > c^*_{NoRat}$. Thus, it does not hold in general that rationing reduces the optimal fleet size.*

Algorithm 4.1 and Equations (4.1), (4.5), and (4.6) can easily be calculated with spreadsheet software or simple programming languages. Due to the upper bound on the fleet size, the optimal fleet size and the optimal threshold level can be found with standard optimization procedures. In the next section, we give a numerical example of the proposed optimization algorithm and compare the results with the results of the policy without rationing.

4.5 Numerical Results

How much can be gained from rationing? What rental fleets are likely candidates for rationing? How does rationing affect capital investments? In this section we perform numerical experiments to obtain answers to these and other questions around our rental system. For our analyses, we use parameter settings that are based on car types of the rail cargo company that motivated our research. At first,

Param.	λ_1	λ_2	q_1	q_2	$\overline{S}$
Type	[orders/day]		[cars/order]		[days]
1	0.50	2.10	20.9	20.9	12.7
2	0.20	0.70	18.6	18.6	16.4
3	0.96	0.64	29.1	24.7	13.57
4	1.02	1.25	9.2	9.5	9.31
5	0.22	0.33	1.8	2.7	11.2
6	0.35	0.65	2.5	3.1	9.1
7	0.43	0.55	1.5	2.8	16.6
8	0.59	1.13	1.2	1.4	24.1
9	5.85	8.79	2.2	1.8	16.9
10	0.11	0.93	20.3	25.6	11.8
11	0.60	3.41	1.4	3.9	9.0
12	0.68	0.84	11.5	13.9	5.0
13	0.30	0.71	15.1	17.0	8.4
14	0.32	0.48	22.7	22.5	13.3
15	1.01	1.53	23.2	22.7	5.2

Table 4.1: Operational parameters of the rail cars analyzed

we introduce fifteen car types and for each car type derive the optimal profit with rationing and without rationing. Afterwards, we analyze how the optimal profit and the optimal fleet size react to changes in mean order sizes, unit penalty cost, and unit holding cost. Finally, we summarize the main insights.

Base Case Optimization Tables 4.1 and 4.2 give, respectively, the operational and cost parameters of the fifteen car types we analyze. We assume a geometric distribution with mean q_i for class i order sizes, because the geometric distribution fitted best the observed order size distribution at the rail cargo company.

For each car type, we first optimize the fleet size and the threshold level. Then, we optimize fleet size in the case without rationing, i.e., with $T = c$, to benchmark the results. The results, the expected daily profits, and the return-on-sales (ROS) for each car type are given in Table 4.3. The column Δ shows the percentage increase in daily profits when changing from no rationing to rationing.

We can see from Table 4.3 that the average increase in profit is about 17%. However, it varies considerably between car types. For car type 10, it is only 2%, while for car type 4 it is as high as 567%. We can observe that the values of Δ

Param.	r_1	r_2	p	h
Type	[Euro]		[Euro]	[Euro/year]
1	758	191	1,300	4,500
2	550	250	250	4,700
3	400	175	750	3,700
4	300	125	650	4,400
5	350	200	850	4,500
6	325	175	725	4,200
7	375	175	675	3,800
8	450	250	1,050	4,100
9	500	250	1,200	4,000
10	400	225	900	4,500
11	350	125	450	4,000
12	150	100	350	4,000
13	300	150	1,000	4,500
14	325	150	600	3,500
15	200	75	550	4,300

Table 4.2: Cost parameters of the rail cars analyzed

	With rationing				Without rationing			
	c^*	T^*	Π	*ROS*	c^*_{NoRat}	Π_{NoRat}	*ROS*	Δ
Type	[cars]	[cars]	[Euro]		[cars]	[Euro]		
1	669	603	5,582	40%	834	4,781	31%	17%
2	237	216	648	17%	269	567	13%	14%
3	21	17	−91	−40%	23	−96	−38%	5%
4	39	33	11	2%	42	2	0%	567%
5	31	19	−82	−28%	44	−124	−30%	33%
6	38	27	−59	−14%	63	−149	−23%	61%
7	487	475	4,585	46%	535	4,319	42%	6%
8	734	607	5,117	39%	819	4,691	35%	9%
9	207	170	1,041	28%	258	769	19%	35%
10	323	313	851	17%	333	833	16%	2%
11	105	103	345	23%	116	321	20%	7%
12	123	99	30	2%	141	−52	−3%	157%
13	175	145	274	10%	203	132	4%	108%
14	269	209	398	12%	326	187	5%	113%
15	364	283	1,709	27%	445	1,269	18%	35%

Table 4.3: Optimal fleet sizes and threshold levels with expected profit

are high if ROS is close to zero. This is, because for fleets with high Δ, a small increase in revenues leads to a large percentage increase in profit. We can also see from Table 4.3 that for all of the fifteen base cases, the optimal fleet size with rationing is less than the optimal fleet size without rationing. Although we have shown in Example 4.1 that this does not hold in general, we see that it is likely for realistic parameter settings. Next, we analyze the effect of order size means, unit penalty cost, and unit holding cost on the optimal profit and the optimal fleet size. For these analyses, we focus on the first four car types, which represent a broad diversity of arrival rates, order sizes, and cost parameters.

Effect of Class 1 Mean Order Sizes on System Performance In this experiment, we vary the mean order size of class 1 demand (q_1) while keeping the total mean of class 1 demand ($\lambda_1 q_1$) constant. We cover a range of $q_1 = 1$ to $q_1 = 40$. Figure 4.2 shows the optimal expected profit with rationing (black line with triangles) and without rationing (grey line with circles) for car types 1 to 4. Figure 4.3 shows the optimal fleet sizes for the case with rationing (grey line with circles) and the case without rationing (black line with triangles) and the optimal threshold level in the case with rationing (grey line with stars) for all four car types.

We can observe on the diagrams of Figure 4.2 that the expected profit decreases in the mean order size of class 1 demand. This result supports the intuitive idea that more demand variability (which is a consequence of larger order sizes) leads to lower expected profit. The percentage decrease in expected profit in the case with rationing by increasing q_1 from $q_1 = 1$ to $q_1 = 40$ ranges between 31% for car type 1 and 114% for car type 4, which demonstrates that order batching has a substantial effect on the performance of a rental system. We can also observe from Figure 4.2 that the potential of using rationing for medium order sizes is larger than the potential for small order sizes. However, the potential does not grow in general, as can be seen at car type 2 where it is decreasing if q_1 is greater than 25.

From Figure 4.3 can be seen that, while expected profit decreases, the optimal

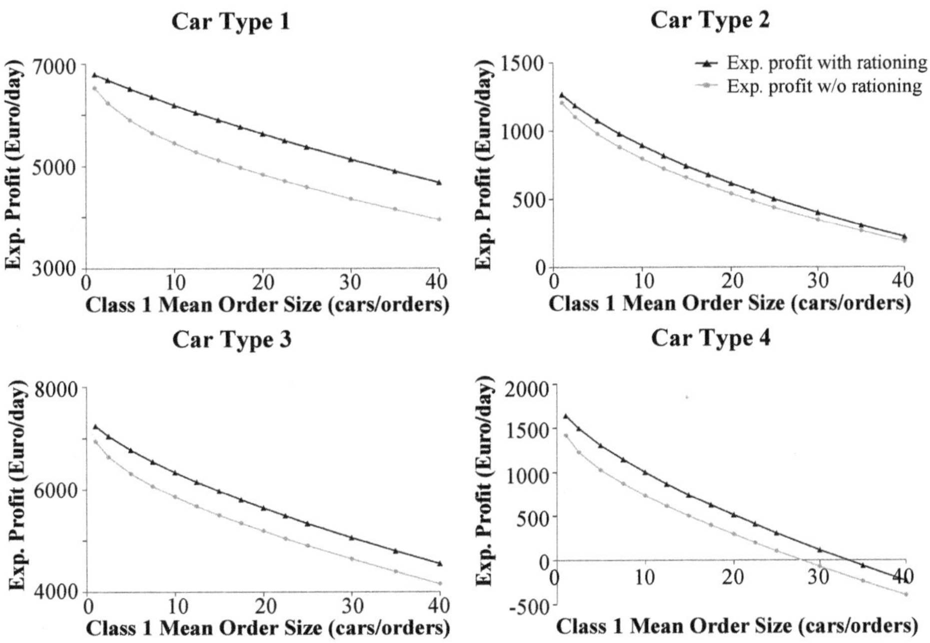

Figure 4.2: Optimal expected profits by class 1 mean order size

fleet size increases in q_1. This seems to hold for the case with rationing as well as for the case without rationing. The threshold level increases slower than the optimal fleet size such that the term $c^* - T^*$ also increases in q_1. This is intuitive, because we need to reserve more cars for class 1 orders to cover the increased variability in class 1 demand. With q_1 close to 1, $c^* - T^*$ is even as small as 2 (car type 2) and 3 (car type 1) cars.

Effect of Class 2 Mean Order Sizes on System Performance Next, we vary the mean order size of class 2 demand (q_2) while keeping the total mean of class 2 demand ($\lambda_2 q_2$) constant. Again, we cover the range between $q_2 = 1$ and $q_2 = 40$. Figure 4.4 shows the optimal expected profit, Figure 4.5 shows the optimal fleet sizes and the optimal threshold level.

From Figure 4.4, we can observe that expected profit decreases in q_2. However, the slope is less steep than with q_1. The percentage decrease in expected profit

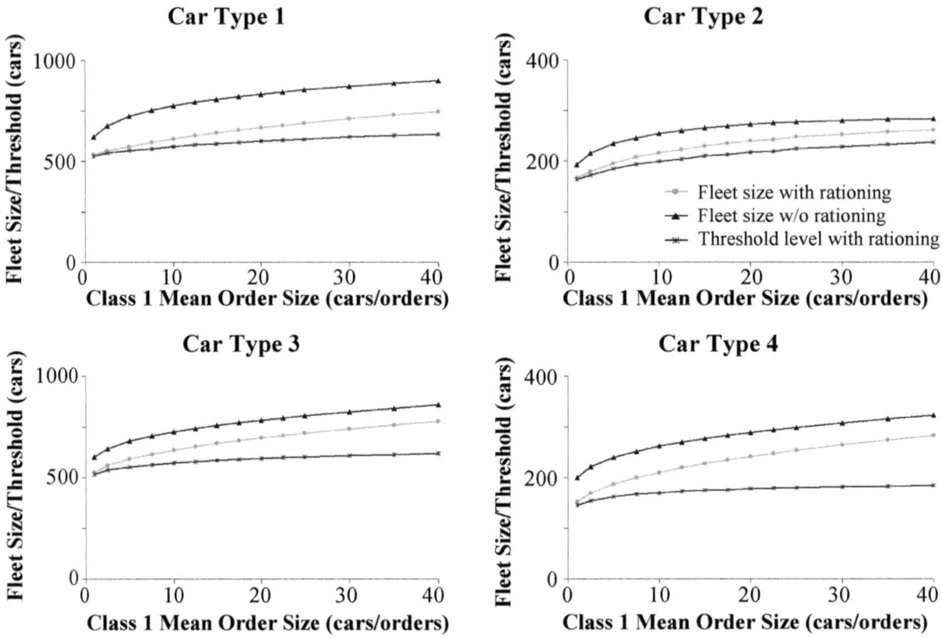

Figure 4.3: Optimal fleet sizes and threshold level by class 1 mean order size

in the case with rationing by increasing q_2 from $q_2 = 1$ to $q_2 = 40$ ranges only between 4% for car type 3 and 38% for car type 2. Thus, in our experiments, batching low-priority demand has less effect on optimal profit than batching high-priority demand. Concerning the potential of rationing, we can make the same observation as in the previous experiment. The potential is larger with batch arrivals than without batch arrivals.

The effect of q_2 on the optimal fleet sizes is different from the effect of q_1 on the optimal fleet sizes (see Figure 4.5). With increasing q_2, the optimal fleet size in the case with rationing decreases. The same holds for the optimal fleet size without rationing, except for car types 1, 3, and 4 where the fleet sizes first increase with low values of q_2. This is interesting, because it is contrary to the effect of q_1 and because we would intuitively expect that more demand variability would again lead to larger optimal fleet sizes. Apparently, variability in class 2 demand reduces

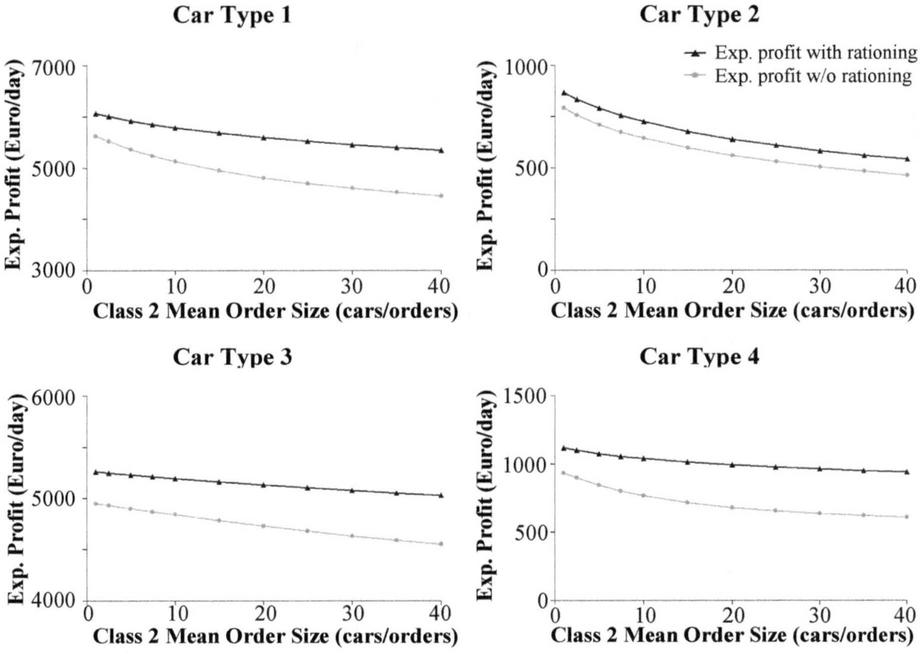

Figure 4.4: Optimal expected profits by class 2 mean order size

utilization of the cars so that holding the same number of cars as with less class 2 demand variability is less profitable than having fewer cars.

Effect of Unit Penalty Cost on System Performance We analyze the effect of the unit penalty cost p on optimal expected profit and on the optimal decision variables by varying p from 50% to 300% of the penalty cost of the base case. Figure 4.6 shows optimal expected profits, Figure 4.7 shows the optimal fleet sizes and the optimal threshold level.

Figure 4.6 reveals that expected profit decreases with increasing p. However, expected profit in the case without rationing decreases faster than expected profit in the case with rationing. Thus, the potential of using rationing increases with increasing p. This result is intuitive, because large penalties lead to greater differences between the customer classes and therefore it becomes more important to treat both demand classes differently. Figure 4.7 gives additional insight into this

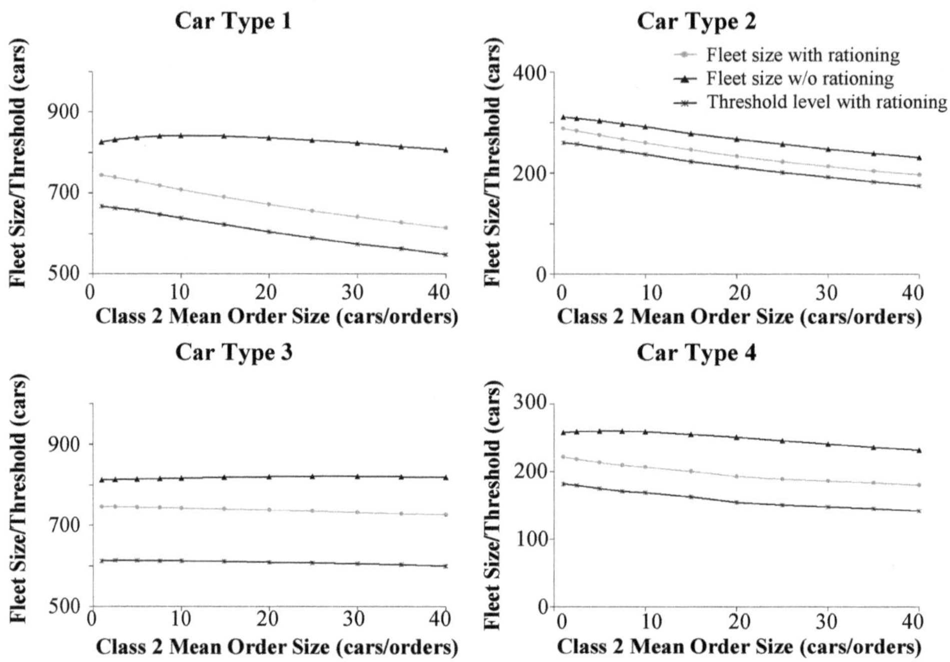

Figure 4.5: Optimal fleet sizes and threshold level by class 2 mean order size

observation. We can see from the optimal fleet sizes that the increasing potential of using rationing is realized by saving holding costs. The fleet size in the case with rationing increases more slowly in p than the optimal fleet size in the case without rationing.

Effect of Unit Holding Cost on System Performance In the final experiment, we vary the unit holding cost h, covering a range between 20% and 200% of the unit holding cost of the corresponding base cases. Figure 4.8 gives the optimal expected profits, Figure 4.9 shows the optimal fleet sizes and the optimal threshold level.

With small values of h optimal fleet sizes are large, because capacity is comparatively inexpensive (see Figure 4.9). Therefore, the system can afford enough cars to fill most demands and rationing is of less importance. This is reflected in the negligible difference between expected profit in the case with rationing and the

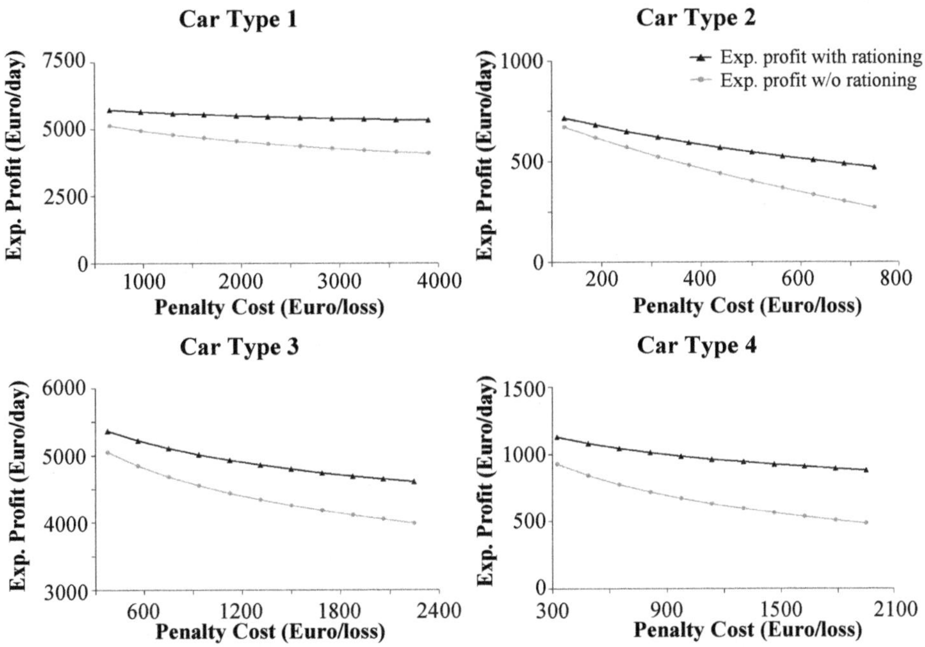

Figure 4.6: Optimal expected profits by unit penalty cost

case without rationing for low holding costs (see Figure 4.8). With increasing unit holding cost, expected profit decreases, but expected profit in the case without rationing decreases faster than in the case with rationing. Thus, the potential of rationing increases with increasing h. The more expensive the cars become, the more important it becomes to optimally utilize the cars. However, the optimal fleet size reaches the lower bound of $c^* = 0$ at some point. This is the case with car type 2 and unit holding costs above $8,000$ Euros per car and year (see Figure 4.8). Therefore, the potential of rationing does not increase in h for all parameter settings. Figure 4.9 shows that the optimal fleet size in the case with rationing decreases faster, in most settings analyzed, than the optimal fleet size in the case without rationing. Thus, the system with rationing is superior to the model without rationing in avoiding excessive fleet holding costs by better utilizing smaller fleets.

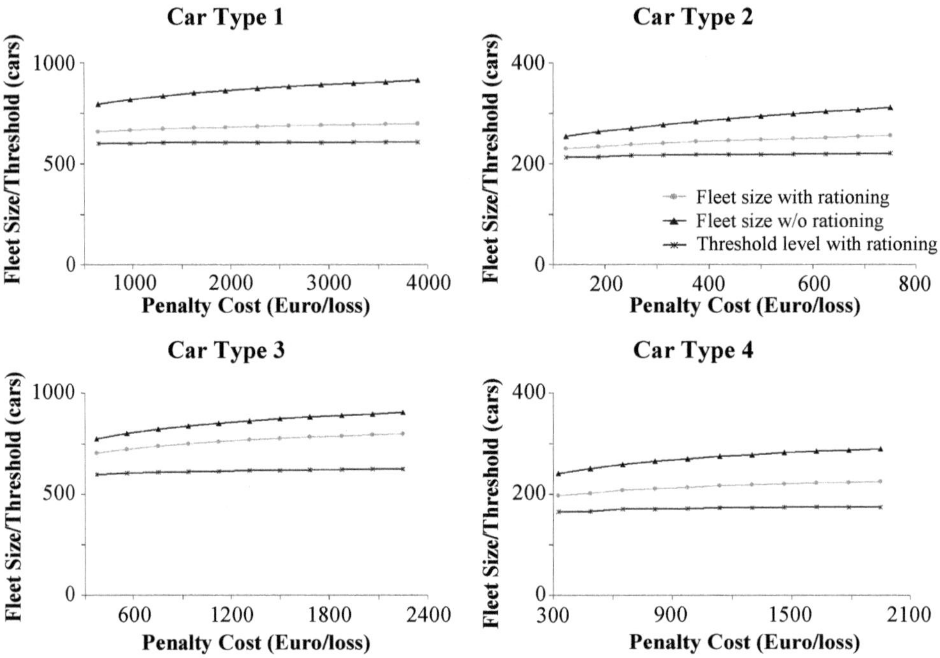

Figure 4.7: Optimal fleet sizes and threshold level by unit penalty cost

Managerial Insights from Numerical Experiments We optimized fleet sizes of fifteen car types and varied system parameters for four car types. Based on our observations, we derive some insights into our rental system that are useful to decision makers in related rental systems:

Insight 4.1 *Using rationing can significantly improve profit. For the fifteen car types analyzed, the average increase in profit was about* 17%.

Insight 4.2 *It is important to consider batched orders in the demand process, especially for high-priority customers. The effect of large orders on the expected profit is substantial, up to* 114% *for some car types. In addition, batched orders lead to a larger potential in rationing than single orders. Therefore, if order batching is neglected, rationing might not seem beneficial although it is.*

Insight 4.3 *The potential of using rationing is especially high in systems with*

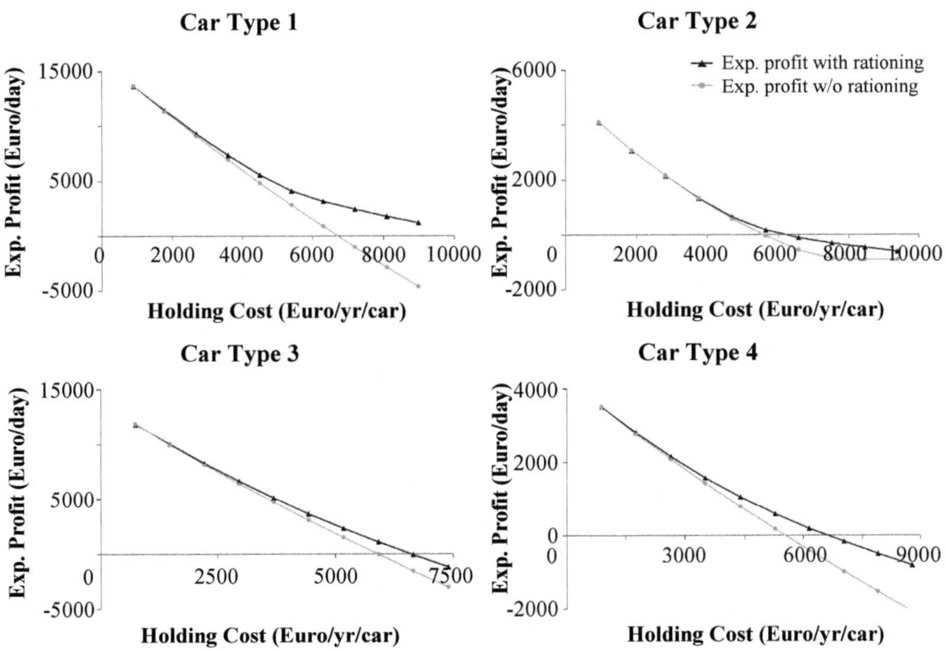

Figure 4.8: Optimal expected profits by unit holding cost

large class 1 order sizes, with large unit penalty cost, and with large unit holding cost. In such systems, introducing rationing to treat customer classes differently is especially worthwhile.

Insight 4.4 *In most realistic settings, using rationing decreases the optimal fleet size. Optimal fleet sizes tend to be especially small in rental systems with small class 1 order sizes or large class 2 order sizes.*

4.6 Conclusion

We analyzed a stochastic rental system in which customers rent batches of rail cars for their transportation demand. The rental company offers two different types of service: Classic service and premium service. Customers of premium service receive an availability guarantee that customers of classic service do not receive.

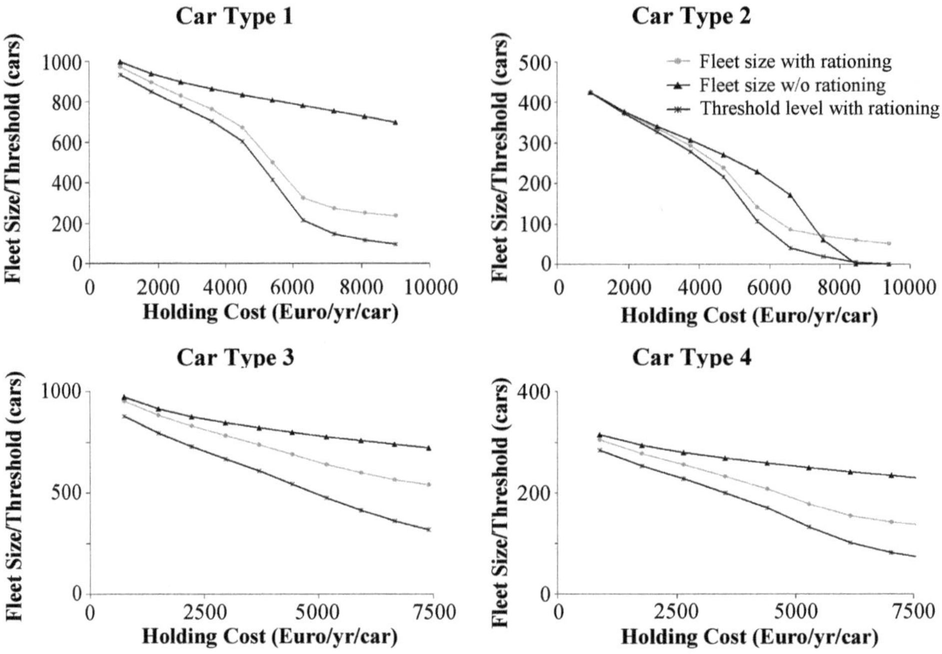

Figure 4.9: Optimal fleet sizes and threshold level by unit holding cost

The rental company can decide on the fleet size that it offers to its customers and about the policy with which it allocates available cars to customer orders. We modeled the rental business as a queuing loss model and showed how to find the joint optimum of fleet size and allocation policy that maximizes expected profit per time unit. Based on these results, we performed numerical experiments with data that is based on fleets from a leading European rail cargo company. From the numerical results, we derived managerial insights into the behavior of the rental system and about the value of using rationing.

The results presented in this chapter can be applied to rental businesses. The optimization method can be used by decision makers, at the same time, to find an optimal allocation of fleet investments and to establish an optimal admission policy to protect high-priority customers. The managerial insights help decision makers to identify rental fleets which are likely to benefit from rationing and they demonstrate that rationing can reduce capital investments. The numerical results also indicated that large order sizes have a substantial effect on the performance of a rental system and that they should be taken into account during fleet planning.

New service models in the B2B rental market are emerging so that further research is necessary to support this development. Recently, advance demand information (ADI) has gained much attention in research and industry practice. In such a setting, customers are required to announce their demand a certain time in advance. These information are likely to improve decision making, however, their presence significantly complicates the analysis of the model.

4.7 Proofs

Proof of Proposition 4.1. Because of the assumption of Poisson distributed demand, an incoming order observes the steady state distribution (PASTA Theorem, cf. Wolff (1989), p. 129). Then, the expected number of served customers per order $E(a^i)$ for a class i order is given by

$$\begin{aligned} E(a^i) &= \sum_{n=0}^{c}\sum_{b=0}^{\infty} P(N=n) f_i(b) E(a^i \mid N=n, B=b) \\ &= \sum_{n=0}^{c}\sum_{b=0}^{\infty} P(N=n) f_i(b) \min([T_i - n]^+, b). \end{aligned} \tag{4.8}$$

Multiplying by the expected number of class i orders per time unit and re-arranging the terms leads to

$$\begin{aligned} V_1(c,T) &= \lambda_1 E(a^1) \\ &= \lambda_1 \sum_{k=0}^{c}\sum_{b=0}^{\infty} P(N=k) f_1(b) \min(b, c-k) \\ &= \lambda_1 \sum_{k=0}^{c} P(N=k) \left(\sum_{b=0}^{c-k} b f_1(b) + (c-k)\overline{F}_1(c-k) \right) \end{aligned} \tag{4.9}$$

for class 1 demand and

$$\begin{aligned} V_2(c,T) &= \lambda_2 E(a^2) \\ &= \lambda_2 \sum_{k=0}^{c} \sum_{b=0}^{\infty} P(N=k) f_2(b) \min(b, [T-k]^+) \\ &= \lambda_2 \sum_{k=0}^{T} P(N=k) \left(\sum_{b=0}^{T-k} b f_2(b) + (T-k) \overline{F}_2(T-k) \right) \end{aligned} \tag{4.10}$$

for class 2 demand with $\overline{F}_i(n) = 1 - F_i(n)$. ∎

Proof of Proposition 4.2. The profit with no cars is $\Pi(0,0) = -p\lambda_1 q_1$. The service rates are bounded above by the respective demands, i.e., $V_1 \leq \lambda_1 q_1$ and $V_2 \leq \lambda_2 q_2$. For a threshold policy, we get

$$\begin{aligned} \Pi(c, T^*(c)) &= r_1 V_1(c, T^*(c)) + r_2 V_2(c, T^*(c)) - p\left(\lambda_1 q_1 - V_1(c, T^*(c))\right) - hc \\ &\leq (r_1 + p)\lambda_1 q_1 + r_2 \lambda_2 q_2 - p\lambda_1 q_1 - hc. \\ &= r_1 \lambda_1 q_1 + r_2 \lambda_2 q_2 - hc. \end{aligned} \tag{4.11}$$

For any fleet size

$$c \geq \frac{(r_1 + p)\,\lambda_1 q_1 + r_2 \lambda_2 q_2}{h}, \tag{4.12}$$

we have

$$\begin{aligned} \Pi(c, T^*(c)) &\leq r_1 \lambda_1 q_1 + r_2 \lambda_2 q_2 - hc \\ &\leq r_1 \lambda_1 q_1 + r_2 \lambda_2 q_2 - h \frac{(r_1 + p)\,\lambda_1 q_1 + r_2 \lambda_2 q_2}{h} \\ &= r_1 \lambda_1 q_1 + r_2 \lambda_2 q_2 - (r_1 + p)\,\lambda_1 q_1 - r_2 \lambda_2 q_2 \\ &= -p\lambda_1 q_1 \end{aligned} \tag{4.13}$$

and, therefore, fleet size c cannot be optimal because the profit is less than with no cars at all ($c = 0$). ∎

Chapter 5

Capacity Rationing under Advance Demand Information

5.1 Introduction

The diversity of customer expectations and the competitive pressure are continuing to increase across industries. Companies are faced with the challenge to offer products and services that are tailored to the needs of their customers and to do so efficiently. To meet this challenge, many companies have started to introduce customer segmentation, an approach where customers are assigned to different classes based on criteria such as revenues, service requirements, or sales volumes. Customers of different classes are then treated differently, e.g., by differentiating services and prices. When customers of several classes demand the same products or services the challenge is to decide which customer demands to fill and which ones to reject. In this chapter, we consider such a situation. We analyze a rental company that operates a common pool of cars to serve two customer classes. The first class of customers requires immediate service, while the second class of customers reserves cars in advance and the company must decide which demands to fill and which ones to reject to maximize expected profit.

The customer segmentation we analyze was motivated by the rail cargo operations of one of Europe's largest logistics service providers. The company owns more

F. Papier, *Optimization of Rental Systems*, Edition KWV,
https://doi.org/10.1007/978-3-658-24313-5_5

than 100 different fleets of cargo rail cars that are rented out to commercial customers. To improve efficiency, the company recently started to differentiate service by offering classic service and premium service. Under *classic service*, customers do not make reservations and the rental service is priced very competitively. However, the company does not guarantee availability of cars. Under *premium service*, customers reserve cars in advance of their demands and receive a service guarantee. These rentals are priced above the price of the classic service. In rare cases in which a premium demand cannot be filled, the customer receives a lump-sum payment from the rail cargo company. Although the premium service is priced above the classic service, it has become quite popular. Customers requiring high availability, such as customers from the automotive industry, and customers who cannot substitute rail cargo transportation by other transportation modes easily, such as the customers from the petrochemical and steel industries, value the availability guarantee and accept the price premium. The challenge of the rail cargo company is deciding which demands to fill and which demands to reject. We have been motivated by this problem and develop and solve a model that addresses the key issues faced by the company. Our objective is gaining general insights into the optimal policy for situations such as the one faced by the rail cargo company.

We are building on two operations research approaches that have recently received a lot of attention. The first approach is admission control in queuing and rental systems, where a decision maker must decide which demands to accept and which demands to reject. The second approach is the use of advance demand information (ADI), where a decision maker‘s objective is taking optimal advantage of information on future demands, such as reservation information. In this chapter, we combine both approaches by analyzing how ADI can be used for admission control in rental systems.

Our main contribution is threefold: Firstly, we derive the structure of the optimal admission policy. Secondly, we propose an ADI policy and show that it generates close-to-optimal results that are, on average, only 0.4% below an upper bound. Thirdly, we demonstrate that the value of ADI can be substantial: In numerical experiments that are based on data from the company that motivated our research the ADI policy increases the return on sales (ROS) by 8%, in an industry where the average ROS is about 3%.

The remainder of the chapter is organized as follows: In Section 5.2, we review the literature. In Section 5.3, we describe the rental model. In Section 5.4, we analyze the structure of the optimal policy and derive lower and upper bounds on the optimal expected profit. Based on the insights we gain from the analyses, we develop a close-to-optimal admission policy in Section 5.5. In Section 5.6, we present numerical results and discuss how the policy reacts to changes in model parameters, such as the demand leadtime. In Section 5.7, we conclude. Section 5.8 contains the proofs.

5.2 Literature Review

Our research is closely related to the literature on admission control in queuing and rental systems and we review this line of literature next. We also build on the literature on inventory rationing and use some concepts from ADI in inventory control. Therefore, we also briefly review the relevant research of these areas.

Research on admission control in queuing and rental systems can be traced back to Miller (1969). He proves the optimality of a threshold policy for a queuing loss system with n customer classes, homogeneous servers, and identical service time distributions for all customers. Several extensions to his model were developed. Lippman (1975) extends the model by allowing customers to wait in a queue with finite capacity. Albright (1977) extends the model to heterogeneous servers. More recently, Altman et al. (2001) continue the analysis by studying admission control in loss systems with compound Poisson arrivals under entire batch blocking. For the special case of two customer classes with Poisson demand, they prove the optimality of threshold policies. Örmeci and Burnetas (2004) extend this result to compound Poisson arrivals and multiple customer classes for identical service time distributions of all customer classes. Most research has concentrated on proving optimality of threshold policies, but not on finding optimal policy parameters. Savin et al. (2005) builds on Altman et al.'s model to analyze stochastic rental systems. They present an approximation for calculating the optimal policy parameters and study the joint optimization of fleet sizes and threshold levels. Wang and Savin (2006) extend the model to a setting where some customers announce an interest in a future demand but do not specify the time of their arrival. Gans and Savin (2007) extend Savin et al.'s model to dynamic pricing. They derive an optimal admission policy for one customer class and optimal prices for the other class.

Another line of literature related to our research is the literature on inventory rationing. Under inventory rationing customers from different customer classes request products from a common inventory. Then, it might be beneficial to reject demand of some low-priority customers and reserve inventory for potential future high-priority customers. Topkis (1968) was among the first authors who studied inventory rationing. His model assumes a periodic-review inventory model with multiple demand classes and lost sales. This work is extended to continuous review systems by Nahmias and Demmy (1981) and Deshpande et al. (2003). Frank et al. (2003) analyze a modification of Topkis' model with two customer classes in which the demand of one customer class must always be filled. Ha (1997) and Ha (2000) analyze inventory rationing in make-to-stock inventory models with several customer classes and lost sales under limited production capacity.

Also relevant to our research is the literature on ADI in inventory control. Most research of this line of literature uses models with a single customer class. Some of the first authors to analyze ADI were Hariharan and Zipkin (1995). They consider a continuous-review inventory model with one customer class where customers place orders in advance. One of their key findings is that using ADI is equivalent to reducing leadtimes. Gallego and Özer (2001) study a related model in a periodic-review setting and prove the optimality of base stock policies. Gallego and Özer

(2003) extend this research to multi-echelon models. Özer and Wei (2004) extend it to limited production capacity. More recently, Marklund (2006) presents a model that allows for heterogeneous customers.

In this chapter, we apply concepts of rationing and ADI to analyze admission control in stochastic rental systems with finite capacity. We go beyond existing research by presenting a model with capacity rationing under ADI, and we show how to exploit the potential of the ADI.

5.3 Model Description

We consider a rental company that operates a fleet of c cars and serves two classes of customers, ADI customers and non-ADI customers. ADI customers reserve cars τ time units before their actual demand occurs and we refer to τ as the demand leadtime. The unit revenue of ADI rentals is r_I. If an ADI demand cannot be filled, the demand is lost and the rental company is charged a unit penalty of p. Non-ADI customers do not make reservations and require immediate service. The unit revenue of non-ADI rentals is r_{II} (with $r_{II} \leq r_I$) and there is no penalty if a non-ADI demand is not filled.

When a demand arrives, a decision maker follows an admission policy Γ and decides to accept or reject the demand. We refer to the corresponding decision variable as a_j, where $a_j = 0$ if the demand of customer j is rejected and $a_j = 1$ if it is accepted. If no car is idle when a customer j arrives, the customer will also be lost and we set $a_j = 0$.

The demand of ADI and non-ADI customers is Poisson distributed with means λ_I and λ_{II}, respectively. Rental times of both customer classes are exponentially distributed with mean $\overline{S}$. Without loss of generality, we set $\overline{S} = 1$ and let λ_I and λ_{II} denote the mean demand during one unit of mean rental time.

Our model closely resembles the operations of the rail cargo company that motivated our research. At the company, customers can order classic or premium service. Under classic service, no reservation is necessary but there is no availability guarantee. Under premium service, which is priced above the classic service, customers order cars about one week in advance and receive an availability guarantee. If a premium demand is not met, customers receive a financial compensation. Similar models with one class of contract customers and one class of walk-in customers, but without ADI, have been analyzed by Frank et al. (2003), Gans and Savin (2007), and Iravani et al. (2007).

The objective of the rental company is to maximize expected profit. The profit is driven by the expected number of customers served, i.e., the *service rate.* We denote the service rates of ADI and non-ADI customers that are served under policy Γ by $V_I(\Gamma)$ and $V_{II}(\Gamma)$, respectively. The expected revenues from ADI and non-ADI demand are $r_I V_I(\Gamma)$ and $r_{II} V_{II}(\Gamma)$, respectively. The expected number of ADI demands that cannot be filled is $\lambda_I - V_I(\Gamma)$ and the corresponding expected penalties are $p(\lambda_I - V_I(\Gamma))$. The expected profit per time unit is equal to the difference in expected revenues and expected penalties:

$$\begin{aligned}\Pi(\Gamma) &= r_I V_I(\Gamma) + r_{II} V_{II}(\Gamma) - p(\lambda_I - V_I(\Gamma)) \\ &= (r_I + p) V_I(\Gamma) + r_{II} V_{II}(\Gamma) - p\lambda_I. \qquad (5.1)\end{aligned}$$

Note that we include in the expected profit function only cost factors that are affected by the admission policy and do not include fixed costs such as the cost of capital of the cars, because these fixed costs are not relevant for the admission policy and we can ignore them in our analysis.

The profit depends on the admission policy through the service rates of ADI and non-ADI demands. To compute the expected profit and to find the optimal policy, we must compute the quantities $V_I(\Gamma)$ and $V_{II}(\Gamma)$, which is analytically intractable. However, we can derive important properties of an optimal policy using stochastic comparisons. We derive these properties in the next section. In the following sections, we build on these properties. We propose an ADI policy and use bounds on the performance of the optimal policy to demonstrate that this ADI policy performs close-to-optimal in several realistic settings.

5.4 Characteristics of the Optimal Policy

We next show that the optimal admission policy is a threshold policy and analyze properties of the optimal threshold levels. It turns out that actually computing the optimal threshold levels is computationally intractable. However, we can derive an upper bound on the performance of the optimal policy that allows us to evaluate the performance of the ADI policy that we propose in the next section. We also derive an optimal non-ADI policy that we use as a benchmark policy in our numerical experiments.

5.4.1 Optimality of Threshold Policy

We denote the number of busy cars by N and the set of ADI customer reservations by $R = \{t_1, t_2, ...\}$, where t_k denotes the time for which customer k demands a car. Since the arrival process is Poisson and the rental times are exponentially distributed, the state space if fully characterized by (N, R). When a demand occurs, a decision maker must decide whether to accept or to reject the demand. If a demand is served, an immediate profit is earned, but one empty car fewer will be available than before. If a demand is rejected, no immediate reward is earned and the number of cars available does not change. The admission policy states under which conditions demands are accepted or rejected. The structure of the optimal admission policy is stated in Proposition 5.1.

Proposition 5.1 *The optimal admission policy is a threshold policy where the threshold level depends on the set of individual reservation times, R.*

All proofs are contained in Section 5.8. Under the threshold policy, a threshold level $T(R)$ is determined for each non-ADI demand such that the demand will only be admitted if the number of busy cars is less than $T(R)$. Note that under the optimal admission policy, the threshold level depends on R, the individual arrival times of the ADI demands within the demand leadtime. In rental models without

ADI, the system is typically fully described by the number of busy cars N and the threshold level T is constant (cf. Savin et al. (2005)).

5.4.2 Properties of Optimal Policy

Under the optimal admission policy, we can decide whether to accept or reject a non-ADI demand based on the number of busy cars N and the set of reservations R. If the immediate revenue that is generated by accepting the demand exceeds the expected future loss in profit of having one car fewer available than if the demand were rejected, than it is optimal to accept the demand. If not, it is optimal to reject it. In this subsection, we derive important properties of the optimal admission policy. These properties give insight into the structure of optimal decisions and we build on them in Section 5.5, when we derive our heuristic ADI policy.

Consider the time at which a demand occurs. Let N^- be the number of cars that are available immediately before the demand occurs and let N^+ be the number of cars that are available immediately after the admission decision has been made. If the demand is rejected, then $N^+ = N^-$. If the demand is accepted, then $N^+ = N^- + 1$. The corresponding difference in expected future profit under the optimal admission policy Γ^* is $E(\Delta\Pi^+(\Gamma^*)) = E(\Pi^+(\Gamma^*) \mid N^+ = N^- + 1, R) - E(\Pi^+(\Gamma^*) \mid N^+ = N^-, R)$.

An important observation will help us understand the structure of the optimal decision. We prove the validity of the observation in the proof of Proposition 5.2 and focus on an intuitive explanation here. Consider two identical systems, X and Y, that face identical arrival and departure processes and that are in an identical state at a time t when a customer arrives. Assume that the customer is accepted at system X and rejected at system Y. At system X, one and only one of the following three events will take place:

Event 1 The accepted customer prevents an ADI customer from entering the system ($\Delta\Pi_1^+ = -(r_I + p)$)

Event 2 The accepted customer prevents a non-ADI customer from entering the system ($\Delta\Pi_2^+ = -r_{II}$)

Event 3 The accepted customer leaves without preventing other customers from entering the system ($\Delta\Pi_3^+ = 0$)

Note that after each of the three events, the states of systems X and Y are identical, because the same number of cars are busy and the same set of reservations is known in both systems. Therefore, the future behavior of systems X and Y will be identical after one of the above events has taken place, and it suffices to analyze the effect of an admission decision on the event probabilities. The three events have different effects on the profit. For given event probabilities, we can calculate the expected future loss from accepting a customer and compare it against the gain in immediate revenues. Based on these observations, we can derive Proposition 5.2.

Proposition 5.2 *For any threshold policy, the optimal decision has the following property*

$$a_j^* = \begin{cases} \mathbf{1}(N^- < c), & r_j - (r_I + p)\, P_1(N^-, R) - r_{II} P_2(N^-, R) > 0 \\ 0, & else. \end{cases} \tag{5.2}$$

The $P_i(N^-, R)$ denote the probabilities that the next event after accepting a customer is rejecting an ADI ($i = 1$) or non-ADI ($i = 2$) customer and r_j denotes the revenue of customer j with $r_j = r_I + p$ if it is an ADI customer and $r_j = r_{II}$ if it is a non-ADI customer.

For ADI customers, it can be immediately seen from $r_j = r_I + p$ and $r_{II} < r_I + p$ that in this case admission $a_j = 1$ is the optimal decision if there is at least one idle car ($N^- < c$). For non-ADI customers, the decision is not as straightforward. If we could compute the probabilities $P_1(N^-, R)$ and $P_2(N^-, R)$, then we could use the results of Proposition 5.2 to determine the optimal policy. However, to compute the probabilities $P_i(N^-, R)$, we must know the optimal policy which we do not know. Therefore, we cannot determine the optimal admission policy. However, we can derive a benchmark policy and an upper bound on the optimal profit.

5.4.3 Optimal Non-ADI Policy as Benchmark

In this section, we derive the optimal policy for the model without ADI. This policy is also feasible under ADI, because the decision maker could simply ignore the ADI. Therefore, it serves as a lower bound on the performance of the optimal policy. Without ADI, the admission decision depends only on N^- and the threshold level is constant. Proposition 5.3 states the result formally and shows how the optimal threshold value can be computed. We note that this policy is a subcase of the rationing policy of Savin et al. (2005).

Proposition 5.3 *Without ADI, the optimal solution is a threshold policy Γ^T with optimal threshold level T^*. T^* can be computed as*

$$T^* = \arg\max_T \left[(r_I + p)V_I(\Gamma^T) + r_{II}V_{II}(\Gamma^T) - p\lambda_I\right], \tag{5.3}$$

with

$$V_I(\Gamma^T) = \lambda_I \left(1 - \frac{\pi_c(\Gamma^T)}{\sum_{k=0}^{c} \pi_k(\Gamma^T)}\right), \text{ and} \tag{5.4}$$

$$V_{II}(\Gamma^T) = \lambda_{II} \left(1 - \frac{\sum_{k=T}^{c} \pi_k(\Gamma^T)}{\sum_{k=0}^{c} \pi_k(\Gamma^T)}\right). \tag{5.5}$$

The probabilities $\pi_k(\Gamma^T)$ are determined by the following set of equations:

$$\begin{aligned}\pi_k(\Gamma^T) &= (\lambda_I + \lambda_{II}\mathbf{1}(k-1<T) + k - 1)\frac{1}{k}\pi_{k-1}(\Gamma^T) \\ &\quad - (\lambda_I + \lambda_{II}\mathbf{1}(k-2<T))\frac{1}{k}\pi_{k-2}(\Gamma^T)\end{aligned} \tag{5.6}$$

for $k = 1...c$ and $\pi_0(\Gamma^T) = 1 - \sum_{k=1}^{c} \pi_k(\Gamma^T)$ (define $\pi_{-1}(\Gamma^T) = 0$).

5.4.4 Upper Bound on Performance of Optimal Policy

We derive an upper bound on the optimal profit by assuming that all future demands are known, ADI demands as well as non-ADI demands. The resulting problem is a stochastic dynamic program. For a given demand realization in interval $[0, \hat{t}]$, it can be solved optimally by backwards recursion.

Let $\widehat{\Pi}\left(\widehat{t}\right)$ denote the expected profit over time interval $\left[0,\widehat{t}\right]$, with $\widehat{t} >> \tau$, and let (A_j, CL_j) denote arrival times (A_j) and class origin pairs $(CL_j \in \{1,2\})$ of all customers, which are assumed to be known. Let j_{max} be the last arrival in this interval and let $\widehat{\Pi}_j^-(k, a_j^*, CL_j)$ and $\widehat{\Pi}_j^+(k)$ denote the future expected profit before and after the arrival of customer j and given that k cars are currently rented out. Then, the optimal admission decision is

$$a_j^* = \begin{cases} \mathbf{1}(k < c) & CL_j = 1 \\ \mathbf{1}(r_{II} + \widehat{\Pi}_j^+(k+1) > \widehat{\Pi}_j^+(k)) & CL_j = 2. \end{cases} \tag{5.7}$$

Assume an arbitrary terminal value $\widehat{\Pi}_{\widehat{t}}^-(k) < +\infty$. The quantities $\widehat{\Pi}^-$ and $\widehat{\Pi}^+$ between arrival times are

$$\begin{aligned} \widehat{\Pi}_j^-(k, a_j^*, CL_j) &= (r_I \mathbf{1}(CL_j = 1) + r_{II}\mathbf{1}(CL_j = 2))\, a_j^* - p\mathbf{1}(a_j^* = 0)\mathbf{1}(CL_j = 1) \\ &\quad + \widehat{\Pi}_j^+(k + a_j^*) \end{aligned} \tag{5.8}$$

and

$$\widehat{\Pi}_j^+(k) = \sum_{n=0}^{k} P(D_j = k - n)\widehat{\Pi}_{j+1}^-(n, a_{j+1}^*, CL_{j+1}), \tag{5.9}$$

where D_j denotes the number of customers returning their cars between arrivals j and $j+1$. Because rental times are exponentially distributed, D_j is a random variable that follows a binomial distribution with k trials and success probability $p = F_S(A_{j+1} - A_j) = 1 - e^{-(A_{j+1} - A_j)}$.

With backward recursion, this problem can be solved optimally. Since all future demands are known, we would intuitively expect that the expected profit is an upper bound on the optimal profit of our original model where only ADI demands within the demand leadtime are known. The following proposition states that this intuition holds.

Proposition 5.4 *The optimal profit for $\widehat{t} \to \infty$ is an upper bound on the optimal* *profit of our rental model, i.e.,*

$$\lim_{\widehat{t}\to\infty} \frac{\widehat{\Pi}(\widehat{t})}{\widehat{t}} \geq \Pi(\Gamma^*). \tag{5.10}$$

Proposition 5.4 holds for an infinite interval length, whereas we must use a finite interval length in our experiments. We will choose $\widehat{t}$ such that the halfwidth of the 95%-confidence interval is less than 0.2% of the mean.

5.5 ADI Policy

We cannot determine the optimal solution, because we cannot determine the probabilities $P_i(N^-, R)$. In the ADI policy we propose in this section, we approximate the probabilities $P_i(N^-, R)$ by assuming that all future admission decisions are made by the threshold policy Γ^T with $T = T^*$ that we introduced earlier. More precisely, for each arrival we assume that this arrival is the only one for which the ADI policy is used. Under this simplifying assumption, we can compute the event probabilities and determine the optimal decision. However, because of this assumption our ADI policy is a heuristic. We next describe the overall structure that we use for estimating the event probabilities (Subsection 5.5.1). Then, we show how the transient behavior of the system between consecutive ADI arrivals can be modeled as a Markov chain (Subsection 5.5.2). Based on the Markov chain representation, we derive expressions for estimating the event probabilities (Subsections 5.5.3 and 5.5.4). Afterwards, we prove that our ADI policy dominates the optimal policy without ADI (Subsection 5.5.5) and describe an algorithm to compute the ADI policy (Subsection 5.5.6). Finally, we illustrate the behavior of the ADI policy with an example (Subsection 5.5.7).

5.5.1 Structure of Event Probabilities

Consider a non-ADI arrival at arrival epoch A_j. Within the demand leadtime τ, i.e., within $]A_j, A_j + \tau]$, we know the arrival epochs of all ADI arrivals. Clearly,

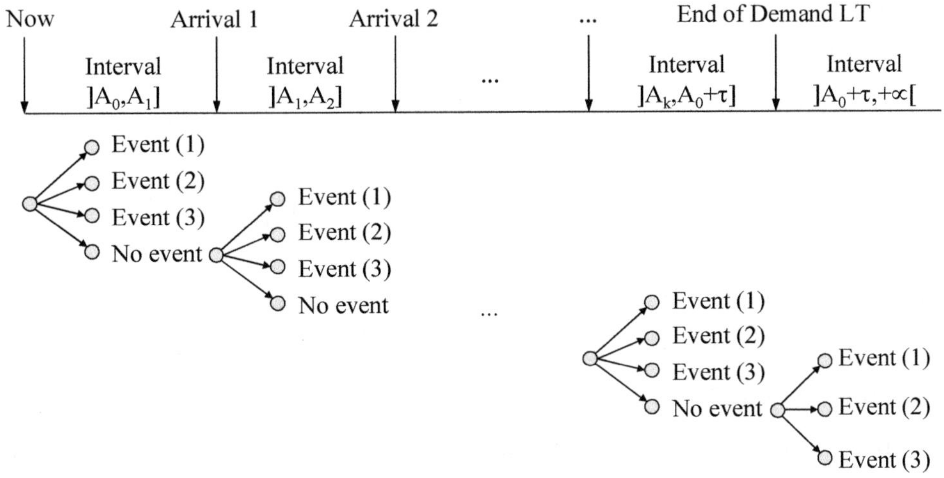

Figure 5.1: Probability tree of non-ADI admission decision

event 1 (accepted customer prevents ADI customer from entering the system) can only occur at beginning or end of an interval, while event 2 (accepted customer prevents non-ADI customer from entering the system) and event 3 (accepted customer leaves without preventing other customers from entering the system) can only occur during an interval. If we knew the distribution of the system state right before all ADI arrivals, we could calculate the probability of event 1 occurring in the demand leadtime. If we further knew the event probabilities in each interval between two consecutive ADI arrivals, we could determine the total probabilities of the events occurring within the demand leadtime. After the demand leadtime, we would have to consider the remaining probabilities of any of the three events. The event structure is presented in the form of a probability tree in Figure 5.1.

From Figure 5.1, we can see that we need the probabilities of all three events for each time interval within the demand leadtime. We denote the event probabilities regarding the jth admission decision in interval $]A_{j+n-1}, A_{j+n}]$ as $p_{1j,n}$, $p_{2j,n}$, and $p_{3j,n}$. From the probabilities within an interval, the overall probabilities of events 1, 2, and 3 can be derived by adding the probabilities of each path of the probability tree (define $\Pi_{j=1}^{0} x(j) = 1$),

$$\begin{aligned} P_i(N_j^-, R_j) &= \sum_{n=1}^{\#R+1} p_{ij,n} \prod_{k=1}^{n-1} \left(1 - p_{1j,k} - p_{2j,k} - p_{3j,k}\right) \\ &\quad + p_{ij,\tau+} \prod_{k=1}^{\#R+1} \left(1 - p_{1j,k} - p_{2j,k} - p_{3j,k}\right). \end{aligned} \tag{5.11}$$

$\#R$ denotes the number of active reservations and $p_{ij,\tau+}$ is the probability of event i occurring after the demand leadtime τ. In Equation (5.11), we sum to $\#R + 1$, because there are $\#R + 1$ intervals in the demand leadtime. The last interval ranges from $A_{\#R}$ to $A_j + \tau$. In the remaining part of the chapter, when referring to the decision about the jth customer, we eventually drop the index j and set $j = 0$. We do this whenever the notation is unambiguous.

Because interarrival times and rental times are exponentially distributed, we can analyze each time interval between two consecutive ADI arrivals separately. Let the distribution right before (after) the arrival of the nth ADI customer be $\boldsymbol{\pi}_n^-$ ($\boldsymbol{\pi}_n^+$). With distribution $\boldsymbol{\pi}_{n-1}^+$ at the beginning of interval n and the transition probabilities during the interval, we can determine distribution $\boldsymbol{\pi}_n^-$ at the end of interval n. Distributions $\boldsymbol{\pi}_{n-1}^+$ and $\boldsymbol{\pi}_n^-$ also determine the interval-specific probabilities p_{1n}, p_{2n}, and p_{3n}. Next, we show how to determine the interval-specific probabilities.

5.5.2 Representation of the System as CTMC

In this subsection, we derive a continuous time Markov chain (CTMC) that describes the transient system behavior between the arrival times of two consecutive ADI customers. Note that we define the CTMC only to model the *difference in system states between having an additional customer and not having one.*

The CTMC has a (finite and discrete) state space of states $0, ..., c$, where c denotes the special, absorbing state when the additional customer has reached threshold T from below. This corresponds to event 2. Event 3 is treated separately. The special state c is absorbing, because after event 2 has occurred, the systems with and without the additional customer will behave identically. We can formulate the infinitesimal generator, $\mathbf{Q}$, as

$$(\mathbf{Q})_{ij} = \begin{cases} \lambda_{II} & i < T-1;\ j = i+1 \\ \lambda_{II} & i = T-1;\ j = c \\ i & 0 < i < c;\ j = i-1 \\ -\sum_{\forall a \neq i} (\mathbf{Q})_{ia} & j = i \\ 0 & otherwise. \end{cases} \tag{5.12}$$

Note that $\mathbf{Q}$ depends only on the parameters c, T, and λ_{II}. If we know $\boldsymbol{\pi}^+_{n-1}$ and given that event 3 has not occurred in the interval, we can calculate $\boldsymbol{\pi}^-_n$ by

$$\boldsymbol{\pi}^-_n = \boldsymbol{\pi}^+_{n-1}\mathbf{P}(A_n - A_{n-1}), \tag{5.13}$$

where $\mathbf{P}(t)$ denotes the transition matrix of the CTMC defined by $\mathbf{Q}$ after t time units. The computationally challenging part is to derive the transition probabilities $\mathbf{P}(t)$ from $\mathbf{Q}$. The transition probabilities are given by $\mathbf{P}(t) = \exp(t\mathbf{Q})$ (cf. Strang (1980), p. 207). Because of the special structure of $\mathbf{Q}$, it is diagonalizable over the real numbers and we use diagonalization to compute $\mathbf{P}(t)$. The structural properties of $\mathbf{Q}$ are stated in the following lemma.

Lemma 5.1 *The generator matrix $\mathbf{Q}$ has real eigenvalues and linearly independent eigenvectors. Therefore, it is diagonalizable over the real numbers.*

By applying diagonalization, $\mathbf{P}(t)$ can be written as

$$\mathbf{P}(t) = \mathbf{U}\mathbf{D}(t)\mathbf{U}^{-1}, \tag{5.14}$$

where $\mathbf{D}(t) = diag(e^{tw_0}, e^{tw_1}, ..., e^{tw_c})$, w_i are the $c+1$ eigenvalues of $\mathbf{Q}$, and $\mathbf{U}$ is the matrix of the (right) eigenvectors corresponding to the eigenvalues as column vectors. From Lemma 5.1, it follows that $\mathbf{U}^{-1}$ exists. Due to the diagonal structure

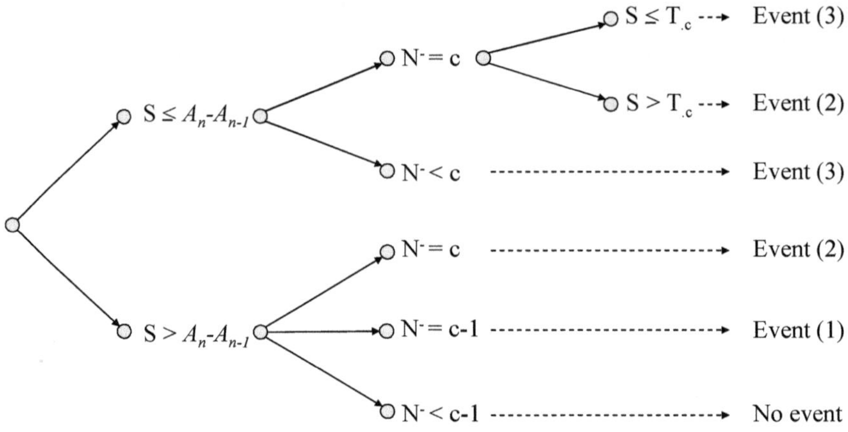

Figure 5.2: Event structure within interval n

of $\mathbf{D}(t)$, the computation of $\boldsymbol{\pi}_n^-$ reduces to

$$\begin{aligned}\left(\boldsymbol{\pi}_n^-\right)_j &= \sum_{i=0}^{c} \left(\boldsymbol{\pi}_{n-1}^+\right)_i (\mathbf{UD}(A_n - A_{n-1})\mathbf{U}^{-1})_{ij} \\ &= \sum_{i=0}^{c} \left(\boldsymbol{\pi}_{n-1}^+\right)_i \sum_{k=0}^{c} \exp\left(\left(A_n - A_{n-1}\right) w_k\right) (\mathbf{U})_{ik} \left(\mathbf{U}^{-1}\right)_{kj}. \quad (5.15)\end{aligned}$$

Next, we need to determine the probabilities within the specific time interval.

5.5.3 Event Probabilities within Demand Leadtime

The event structure within each time interval (including events that occur at the end of the interval) is visualized in Figure 5.2. S denotes the rental time of the additional customer and $T_{.c}$ the first passage time into the absorbing state c. While more than one event might occur within the interval, we let p_{in} denote the probability that event i is the first event to occur in interval n. We can derive the probabilities of events 1, 2, and 3 as stated in the following lemma.

Lemma 5.2 *The probabilities of events $i = 1, 2, 3$ occurring first within or at the* *end of interval n are given by*

$$p_{1n} = e^{-(A_n - A_{n-1})} \left(\boldsymbol{\pi}_n^-\right)_{c-1}, \tag{5.16}$$

$$\begin{aligned} p_{2n} &= e^{-(A_n - A_{n-1})} \left(\boldsymbol{\pi}_n^-\right)_c \\ &+ \sum_{k=0}^{c} \left(\sum_{i=0}^{c} \left(\boldsymbol{\pi}_{n-1}^+\right)_i \mathbf{U}_{ik} \mathbf{U}_{kc}^{-1} \right) \alpha_k (A_n - A_{n-1}), \end{aligned} \tag{5.17}$$

and

$$\begin{aligned} p_{3n} &= 1 - e^{-(A_n - A_{n-1})} \\ &- \sum_{k=0}^{c} \left(\sum_{i=0}^{c} \left(\boldsymbol{\pi}_{n-1}^+\right)_i \mathbf{U}_{ik} \mathbf{U}_{kc}^{-1} \right) \alpha_k (A_n - A_{n-1}), \end{aligned} \tag{5.18}$$

with

$$\alpha_k(x) = \begin{cases} \frac{\left(e^{(w_k - 1)x} - 1\right)}{w_k - 1} & w_k \neq 1 \\ x & w_k = 1. \end{cases} \tag{5.19}$$

If none of the above events occurs, the distribution $\boldsymbol{\pi}_n^+$ is given by

$$\begin{aligned} \left(\boldsymbol{\pi}_n^+\right)_j &= P\left(N^+ = j \mid N^- < c-1\right) \\ &= \begin{cases} \frac{1}{1 - \left(\boldsymbol{\pi}_n^-\right)_{c-1} - \left(\boldsymbol{\pi}_n^-\right)_c} \left(\boldsymbol{\pi}_n^-\right)_{j-1} & 0 < j \leq c-1 \\ 0 & \textit{otherwise.} \end{cases} \end{aligned} \tag{5.20}$$

5.5.4 Event Probabilities after Demand Leadtime

Now, we derive the event probabilities after the demand leadtime, $p_{1,\tau+}$, $p_{2,\tau+}$, and $p_{3,\tau+}$. The behavior after the demand leadtime is relevant, because any of the three events can occur after that time. We will denote the state distribution by $\boldsymbol{\pi}_{\#R+1}$. Since there is no event at the end of the demand leadtime, the before and after distribution are identical and we drop the + and − sign from the notation. The behavior of the system after time $A_0 + \tau$ can be modeled as a CTMC with state space $0, 1, ..., c, c+1, c+2$. We define three artificial, absorbing states (c,

$c+1$, and $c+2$) corresponding to the three events. State c corresponds to event 1, state $c+1$ corresponds to event 2, and state $c+2$ corresponds to event 3. Instead of using the transition function of the CTMC it is more convenient to use the transition matrix of the embedded discrete time Markov chain (eDTMC), because we can then directly derive the event probabilities. Denote the transition matrix of the eDTMC by $\mathbf{P}_{\mathcal{T}+}$. It is straightforward to formulate $\mathbf{P}_{\mathcal{T}+}$:

$$(\mathbf{P}_{\mathcal{T}+})_{ij} = \begin{cases} \frac{\lambda_I+\lambda_{II}}{\delta_i} & i < T-1;\ j = i+1 \\ \frac{\lambda_I}{\delta_i} & T-1 \leq i < c;\ j = i+1 \\ \frac{\lambda_{II}}{\delta_i} & i = T-1;\ j = c+1 \\ \frac{i}{\delta_i} & 0 < i < c;\ j = i-1 \\ \frac{1}{\delta_i} & i < c;\ j = c+2 \\ 1 & i \geq c;\ j = i \\ 0 & otherwise, \end{cases} \tag{5.21}$$

where δ_i are the corresponding weights that normalize each row sum of the matrix to 1. Matrix $\mathbf{P}_{\mathcal{T}+}$ describes an absorbing DTMC. Rewrite $\mathbf{P}_{\mathcal{T}+}$ as

$$\mathbf{P}_{\mathcal{T}+} = \begin{pmatrix} \widetilde{\mathbf{P}} & \mathbf{C} \\ \overline{\mathbf{0}} & \mathbf{I_3} \end{pmatrix} \tag{5.22}$$

with $\mathbf{I_3}$ as the 3×3 identity matrix, $\overline{\mathbf{0}}$ as the $3 \times c$ null matrix, and $\widetilde{\mathbf{P}}$ and $\mathbf{C}$ as the remaining submatrices. Furthermore, let matrix $\mathbf{A}$ denote the probabilities of reaching absorbing state j from transient state i. By Kemeny and Snell (1960), p. 46-55, $\mathbf{A} = (\mathbf{I_c} - \widetilde{\mathbf{P}})^{-1}\mathbf{C}$. With $\mathbf{A}$ known, $p_{1,\mathcal{T}+}$, $p_{2,\mathcal{T}+}$, and $p_{3,\mathcal{T}+}$ can be determined by

$$\begin{aligned} p_{1,\mathcal{T}+} &= \boldsymbol{\pi}_{\#R+1} \cdot (\mathbf{A})_1\,, \\ p_{2,\mathcal{T}+} &= \boldsymbol{\pi}_{\#R+1} \cdot (\mathbf{A})_2\,, \text{ and} \\ p_{3,\mathcal{T}+} &= \boldsymbol{\pi}_{\#R+1} \cdot (\mathbf{A})_3\,. \end{aligned} \tag{5.23}$$

5.5.5 Dominance of ADI Policy over Non-ADI Policies

We can prove that our policy is always superior to a policy in which ADI is not used. Thus, we are always better off to use our sub-optimal ADI policy than to ignore ADI. This result is formally stated in the following proposition.

Proposition 5.5 *The long-run performance of the ADI policy Γ^{ADI} is always greater than or equal to the performance of the best policy without ADI, the state-dependent threshold policy Γ^{T}, i.e.,*

$$\Pi(\Gamma^T) \leq \Pi(\Gamma^{ADI}). \tag{5.24}$$

Next, we describe an algorithm that uses the results from this and the preceding subsections.

5.5.6 Algorithm for Computing ADI Event Probabilities

The results of Section 5.5 allow the computation of the estimates for $P_1(N^-, R)$ and $P_2(N^-, R)$ for each non-ADI arrival. The estimates can then be used for the admission rule of Proposition 5.2.

Algorithm 5.1 *Computation of event probabilities for non-ADI arrival in state* (N^-, R)

- *0. Set* $\widetilde{p} = 1$, $P_i(N^-, R) = 0$ *for* $i = 1, 2, 3$.
- *0b. Set* $\left(\boldsymbol{\pi}_0^+\right)_k = 1$ *for* $k = N_j^-$ *and* $\left(\boldsymbol{\pi}_0^+\right)_k = 0$ *for all other* k.
- *1. Repeat for all reservations in* R, *use index* $n = 1 \ldots.$
  - *1a. Compute* $\boldsymbol{\pi}_n^-$ *with Equation (5.15).*
  - *1b. Compute* p_{1n}, p_{2n}, *and* p_{3n} *with Equations (5.16), (5.17), and (5.18).*
  - *1c. Compute* $\boldsymbol{\pi}_n^+$ *with Equation (5.20).*
  - *1d. Update* $P_i(N^-, R) = P_i(N^-, R) + \widetilde{p} \cdot p_{in}$ *for* $i = 1, 2, 3$.
  - *1e. Update* $\widetilde{p} = \widetilde{p} \cdot (1 - p_{1n} - p_{2n} - p_{3n})$.
- *2. Compute* $\boldsymbol{\pi}_n^-$ *with Equation (5.15) and interval length* $A_0 + \tau - A_{\#R}$.
- *3. Compute* p_{2n} *and* p_{3n} *with Equations (5.16) and (5.18) and set* $p_{1n} = 0$.

4. Copy $\boldsymbol{\pi}_n^-$ *to* $\boldsymbol{\pi}_n^+$.

5. Update $P_i(N^-, R) = P_i(N^-, R) + \widetilde{p} \cdot p_{in}$ *for* $i = 1, 2, 3$.

6. Update $\widetilde{p} = \widetilde{p} \cdot (1 - p_{1n} - p_{2n} - p_{3n})$.

7. Update $P_i(N^-, R) = P_i(N^-, R) + \widetilde{p} \cdot p_{i,\tau+}$ *for* $i = 1, 2, 3$ *with Equation (5.23).*

At each arrival of a non-ADI customer, the algorithm needs to be run on-line to compute the event probabilities for the current system state. The eigenvalues $\{w_i\}$, the matrix of eigenvectors $\mathbf{U}$, its inverse $\mathbf{U}^{-1}$, and matrix $\mathbf{A}$ can be pre-computed during setup of the system, because they do not change during run-time. For all numerical examples in this chapter, the computation time for one decision was significantly less than a second on a standard PC.

5.5.7 Illustration of ADI Policy

In the preceding subsections, we have developed the ADI policy and we have shown that it is superior to policies without ADI. In this subsection, we illustrate the behavior of the ADI policy by providing an example. We show that making decisions based on the number of open reservations is not optimal, but that the individual arrival times have an impact on the quality of the admission decision.

Figure 5.3 shows an example of a threshold level curve of a system with $c = 3$ cars, $\lambda_{II} = 0.225$ cars/days, $\tau = 5$, $r_I = r_{II} = 1.0$, and $p = 0.8$. The triangular marks show times at which ADI customers require a car. The dotted line shows the number of open reservations, i.e., the arrivals of ADI demands within the demand leadtime τ. The solid line represents the threshold level under the ADI policy. In our example, three arrivals occur around $t = 10$, resulting in a reduction of the threshold level from 3 to 0 around $t = 5$. Note that around $t = 5$, the three ADI demands become visible to the decision maker, resulting in an immediate decrease of the threshold level from 3 to 0. The behavior of the policy is different if ADI demands are more widely spread. For instance, consider the three arrivals around $t = 25$. There, time interval $[20, 21]$ and time interval $[21, 22]$ both have two open reservations. However, the threshold level of the first interval is two,

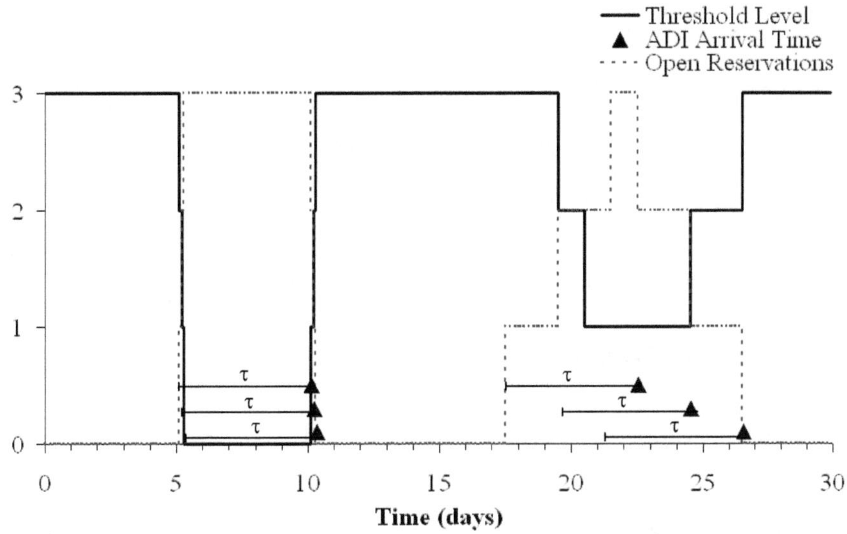

Figure 5.3: Threshold level and number of open reservations by time for sample problem

while the threshold level of the second interval is one, because the second interval is closer to the next two ADI demands. Thus, admitting a non-ADI demand in the second interval is likely to have a bigger effect on the two ADI demands that are within the demand leadtime. The behavior is also different in time intervals $[22, 23]$ and $[23, 25]$. Both time intervals have an identical threshold level of 1. However, in interval $[22, 23]$ three reservations are open while in interval $[23, 25]$ only two reservations are open. The reason is that the last two ADI demands are closer to interval $[23, 25]$ than to interval $[22, 23]$, which offsets the effect of the additional ADI demand that is visible to the decision maker in interval $[22, 23]$. The example demonstrates that the individual arrival times have an effect on the threshold level. Therefore, the admission policy must take these individual arrival times into account.

Param.	Units	Type 1	Type 2	Type 3	Type 4
λ	cars/day	1.29	2.85	2.11	2.35
v^1	%	30	30	30	30
$\overline{S}$	days	11.2	9.1	16.6	24.1
c	cars	12	22	30	48
r_I	Euro/rental	350	325	375	450
r_{II}	Euro/rental	200	175	175	250
p	Euro/loss	850	725	675	1,050

[1] $v = \lambda_I/(\lambda_I + \lambda_{II})$

Table 5.1: Parameter values used in the experiments

5.6 Numerical Results

In this section, we report the results of numerical experiments. We are primarily interested in answering two questions: (a) In which situations is using ADI particularly beneficial and in which is it not? (b) How well does our ADI policy perform? To answer these questions we define four base cases that are based on the rail car fleets of the rail cargo company, where each base case corresponds to a car type that is currently operated by the company. Types 1 and 4 are closed hopper cars with bogies. Type 1 is mainly used for loose bulk such as gravel and coal, type 4 is mainly used for heavy packaged goods. Type 2 is a flat car with bogies that transports steel coils. Type 3 is an open hopper car that is primarily used for loose bulk goods. For the base cases, we use a demand leadtime of one week ($\tau = 7$ days). All other fleet parameters of the four car types are presented in Table 5.1.

We simulate the performances of our ADI policy (ADIP), the benchmark policy without ADI (BMP), and the upper bound (UB) for each car type. In all experiments, we use 20 replications with replication lengths of 1,000 mean rental times plus warm-up periods, resulting in widths of the 95% confidence intervals of less than 0.5% of the mean.

Base Cases The results of the four base cases are shown in Table 5.2. We can see that the service rates of the ADI policy are always greater than the service rates of the benchmark policy. Note that the ADI potential is realized by increas-

	Type 1			Type 2		
	BMP	ADIP	UB	BMP	ADIP	UB
Service Rates [cars/day]						
ADI Demand	0.368	0.377	0.379	0.842	0.846	0.848
Non-ADI Demand	0.454	0.473	0.472	1.119	1.219	1.219
Service Levels [%]						
ADI Demand	95.1	97.4	97.9	98.5	98.9	99.2
Non-ADI Demand	50.3	52.4	52.3	56.1	61.1	61.1
Rev./Costs [Euro/day]						
Revenues	219.5	226.6	226.8	469.4	488.4	488.9
Penalties	16.1	8.5	7.2	9.5	6.3	5.2
Profit	**203.4**	**218.1**	**219.6**	**459.9**	**482.1**	**483.7**

	Type 3			Type 4		
	BMP	ADIP	UB	BMP	ADIP	UB
Service Rates [cars/day]						
ADI Demand	0.625	0.627	0.627	0.698	0.702	0.702
Non-ADI Demand	0.907	0.957	0.962	1.084	1.110	1.118
Service Levels [%]						
ADI Demand	98.7	99.1	99.1	99.0	99.6	99.6
Non-ADI Demand	61.4	64.8	65.1	65.9	67.5	68.0
Rev./Costs [Euro/day]						
Revenues	393.2	402.4	403.5	585.3	593.6	595.2
Penalties	5.3	4.3	4.2	6.9	2.8	3.6
Profit	**387.9**	**398.1**	**399.3**	**578.4**	**590.8**	**591.6**

Table 5.2: Expected profit of the four base cases

ing revenues as well as saving penalties. Apparently, the ADI policy is superior to the benchmark policy in admitting more non-ADI demands as well as in avoiding losses of ADI demands. We can also observe that the service levels of ADI demands are high, well above 90%, while the service levels of non-ADI demands are comparatively low, below 70%. This reflects the unbalanced profitability of the two demand classes. Next, we study the effect of the system parameters that can be controlled by the rental company, i.e., the penalty cost p, the fleet size c, and the demand leadtime τ, on the performance of the rental system. In each experiment, we vary one parameter at a time, keeping all other parameters constant.

Effect of Penalty Cost on Expected Profit We vary the penalty costs around our base cases by increasing and decreasing them by 75%. The results are shown in Figure 5.4 and indicate that our ADI policy performs close to the upper bound and, therefore, close to optimal. As expected, profit decreases in the penalty cost. This is intuitive, because the rental company has to pay more for each ADI demand not filled if the penalty cost increases. What is more interesting is the observation that the performance of the benchmark policy (which also serves as a lower bound) seems to decrease faster than the upper bound and than the profit of the ADI policy. This observation indicates that the potential of using ADI as well as the advantage of the ADI policy over traditional policies increases in the penalty cost p. Using the ADI policy is therefore more useful if the penalty cost is high than if it is low. This result is reasonable, because avoiding lost ADI demand becomes more important when the penalty for it is high. Equation (5.1) shows that a difference in class revenues has a similar effect. Thus, a big difference in class revenues also leads to a high ADI potential.

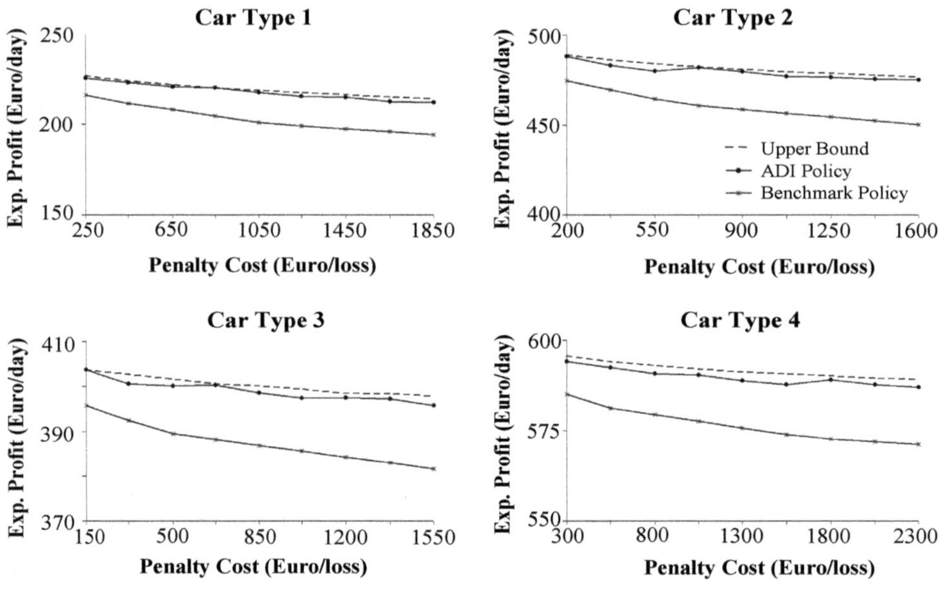

Figure 5.4: Expected profit as a function of the penalty cost

Effect of Fleet Size on Expected Profit We analyze the impact of the fleet size c on performance by increasing and decreasing the fleet sizes around the base cases in step sizes of one car for car types 1 and 2 and step sizes of two cars for car types 3 and 4. The results are summarized in Figure 5.5. Again, we can observe that for all fleet sizes, the ADI policy achieves a performance that is close to the upper bound and, therefore, close to optimal. We can further see that the potential of ADI decreases in the fleet size. This is intuitive, because the more cars are available the fewer demands are lost. With fewer demands lost, rationing is less important than with more demands lost.

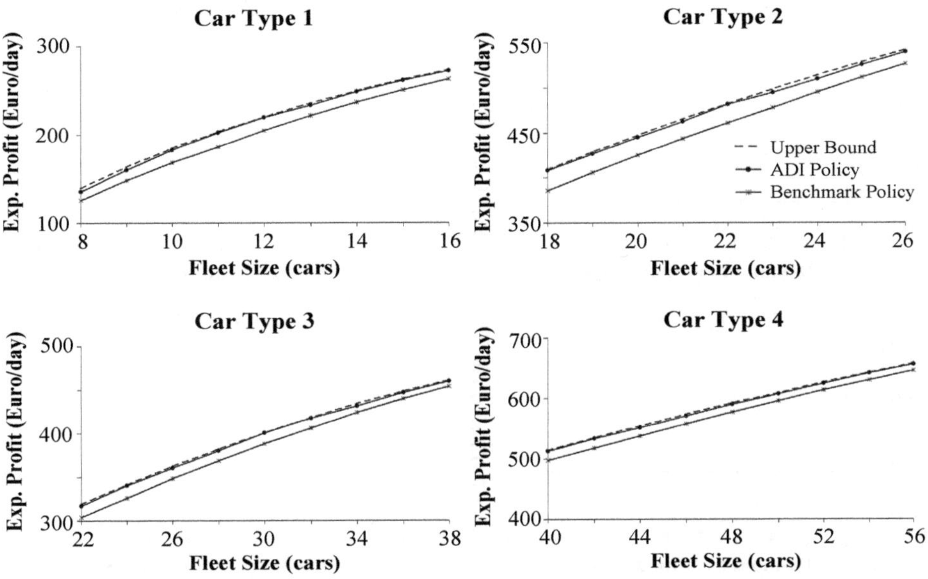

Figure 5.5: Expected profit as a function of the fleet size

Effect of Demand Leadtime on Expected Profit In our final experiment, we study the impact of the demand leadtime on performance by varying the demand leadtime from $\tau = 0$ days to $\tau = 10$ days. The results for each of the four car types are shown in Figure 5.6. As can be seen from the figures, there is a comparatively steep increase in profit for demand leadtimes of up to 5 days. For demand leadtimes greater than 5 days, the profit remains relatively constant. This is interesting, because it shows that it is not necessary to have long demand leadtimes, but that there seems to be a certain limit after which increasing the demand leadtime further has little impact on profit. For short demand leadtimes, the performance of our ADI policy is far below the upper bound. This does not necessarily imply that it is far below optimality. For instance for a demand leadtime of $\tau = 0$, the benchmark policy is optimal and our ADI policy achieves the same performance. Note that the profit is not necessarily strictly monotone in the demand leadtime, because our ADI policy is a heuristic.

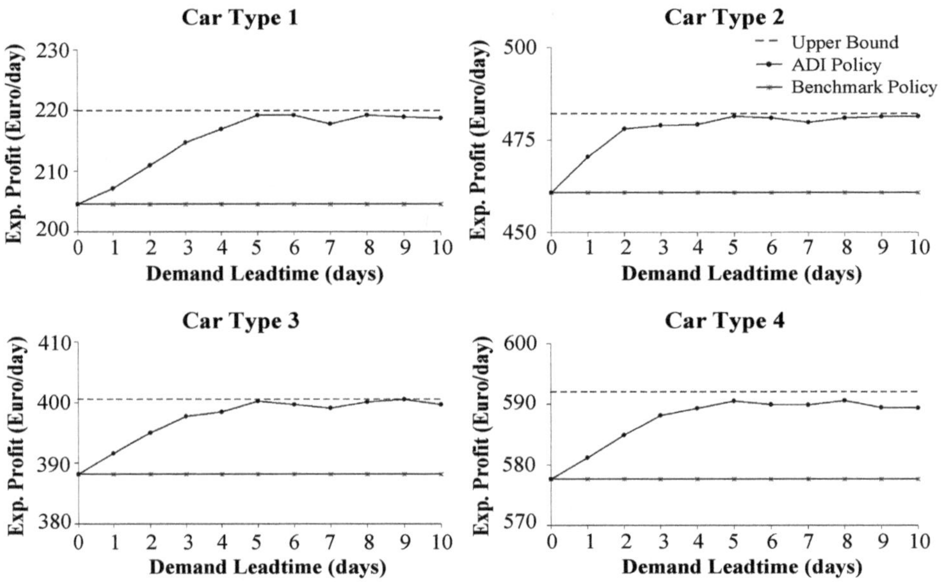

Figure 5.6: Expected profit as a function of the demand leadtime

The numerical experiments give insight into the questions that we posed at the beginning of the section. The potential of using ADI can be substantial. For our four base cases, it increases return on sales (ROS) between 2.3% (car type 4) and 8.0% (car type 1), which is substantial in an industry with an average ROS of about 3%. The benefit of the ADI policy is particularly high in situations with high penalty costs and high differences in class revenues. If ADI is available, our ADI policy utilizes the largest part of its benefit. Table 5.2 and the diagrams reveal that the profit of the ADI policy is very close to the upper bound, which implies that it performs close to optimal. For the base cases, the results of the ADI policy were on average 0.4% below the upper bound. Demand leadtimes have a major effect on the profit. However, for the cases analyzed, demand lead times of 5 days were sufficient to capture most of the maximum value of ADI.

We conclude that using ADI is an important approach to substantially improve profits and that our ADI policy achieves results which are very close to optimality.

5.7 Conclusion

We analyzed a rental model with two customer classes, where one class of customers provides ADI and the other one does not provide ADI. The model was motivated by a new service offered by one of Europe's largest rail cargo companies. We analyzed the structure of the optimal admission policy and proved that the optimal admission policy is a threshold policy. Since it was numerically intractable to compute the optimal policy, we developed a close-to-optimal policy, the ADI policy. We also developed a lower bound and an upper bound on the optimal expected profit. The bounds were used to demonstrate the potential benefit of using ADI and to assess the quality of the ADI policy. We could also analytically prove that our ADI policy always outperforms policies that ignore ADI. The analysis was supported by numerical experiments. The parameters for the numerical experiments were based on fleets of cargo rail cars from the company that motivated our research. The experiments confirmed that ADI can significantly improve profit, between 2.3% and 8.0% for the base cases analyzed. We also showed that the performance of our ADI policy is close to optimal, with an average performance of 0.4% below the upper bound for the test cases analyzed.

The results in this chapter can be used by decision makers of rental businesses to exploit the value of ADI. As we have demonstrated, ADI can lead to significant profit improvements and the ADI policy developed in this chapter realizes most of this potential. The ADI policy can be implemented on standard PCs and used in real time.

We have analyzed the case in which ADI customers pay an additional premium for the availability guarantee. In other settings, ADI customers may pay less than non-ADI customers as a reward for the additional information they provide. In such a case, it might not be optimal to fill all ADI demands and it would be interesting to analyze these settings. Another interesting setting is a rental system in which ADI customers, upon reservation, announce their anticipated rental time in addition to their arrival time. These information could be used to improve decision making. Since both modifications result in quite different models and analyses, we leave them for further research.

5.8 Proofs

Proof of Proposition 5.1. Let $\Pi_j^+(k)$ denote the optimal future profit of a rental system with currently k busy cars and reservation information R right after arrival j. *Note that $\Pi_j^+(k)$ is, in this proof, a random variable.* We show that

$$\Pi_j^+(k+2) - \Pi_j^+(k+1) \leq_{st} \Pi_j^+(k+1) - \Pi_j^+(k), \ \forall k = 0...c-2, \tag{5.25}$$

from which follows that $E\left(\Pi_j^+(k)\right)$ is concave in $k = 0...c-2$. With $E\left(\Pi_j^+(k)\right)$ being concave in k, $E\left(\Delta\Pi_j^+(k)\right)$ is decreasing in k. Thus, if $E\left(\Delta\Pi_j^+(k)\right) < -r_j$ for some k, it would be optimal to reject customer k and it would also be optimal for all $k' > k$ (because $E\left(\Delta\Pi_j^+(k)\right)$ is decreasing). The smallest k for which we would reject a non-ADI customer is the threshold level. This level may not be static but depends on the available ADI, R. Since the demand processes are stationary, it is obvious that if the system has the same ADI at two different time epochs, the threshold levels at the two time epochs will be identical. Thus, the threshold level can *only* depend on R.

Given a certain action a_{j+1}, we get

$$\Pi_j^+(k|a_{j+1}) = r_{j+1}a_{j+1} + \Pi_{j+1}^+(k - D_j + a_{j+1}) \tag{5.26}$$

with D_j as the departures in time period $[A_j, A_{j+1}]$.

Now, we consider four systems $\mathcal{S}1$, $\mathcal{S}2$, $\mathcal{S}3$, and $\mathcal{S}4$ with identical arrival processes (and, thus, all systems have the same ADI). The systems have the respective system states $k+2$, k, $k+1$, $k+1$. The departure probability of the first additional customer in $\mathcal{S}1$ and the additional one in $\mathcal{S}3$ are identical. Therefore, we couple these two events and denote the corresponding random variable of the customer still being in the system with N' ($N'=0$ corresponds to a departure of this customer, $N'=1$ means that the customer is still in the system). We also couple the departure event of the second additional customer in $\mathcal{S}1$ and the departure event of the additional customer in $\mathcal{S}4$. We call the corresponding random variable N''. Let systems $\mathcal{S}1$ and $\mathcal{S}2$ behave optimally, while systems $\mathcal{S}3$ and $\mathcal{S}4$ take their actions based on the system states and the prior departure events.

Now assume we are at the last arrival j_{max}. In this period, the terminal value is identical for all system states (by assumption), i.e., we have

$$\Pi^{+}_{j_{\max}}(k+2) + \Pi^{+}_{j_{\max}}(k) - \Pi^{+}_{j_{\max}}(k+1) - \Pi^{+}_{j_{\max}}(k+1) = 0, \ \forall k = 0 \ldots c-2 \quad (5.27)$$

and Ineq. (5.25) holds for $j = j_{max}$.

Next, we proceed by backward induction on arrival j. Assume that Ineq. (5.25) holds for $j+1$ (as we have shown for j_{max}). A consequence from this is that the optimal decisions of $\mathcal{S}1$ and $\mathcal{S}2$ are related: $a_{j+1}(\mathcal{S}1) \leq a_{j+1}(\mathcal{S}2)$. We assume an arbitrary system state k and distinguish between two cases:

Case 1. $a_{j+1}(\mathcal{S}1) = a_{j+1}(\mathcal{S}2) = a$. In this case, let systems $\mathcal{S}3$ and $\mathcal{S}4$ take the same actions at $j+1$ as $\mathcal{S}1$ and $\mathcal{S}2$. Then, we have for arrival j,

$$\begin{aligned}
& \Pi_j^+(k+2) + \Pi_j^+(k) - \Pi_j^+(k+1|a_{j+1}(\mathcal{S}3)=a) \\
& \quad - \Pi_j^+(k+1|a_{j+1}(\mathcal{S}4)=a) \\
=_{st} \quad & r_{j+1}a + \Pi_{j+1}^+(k+N'+N''-D_j+a) \\
& + r_{j+1}a + \Pi_{j+1}^+(k-D_j+a) \\
& - r_{j+1}a - \Pi_{j+1}^+(k+N'-D_j+a) \\
& - r_{j+1}a - \Pi_{j+1}^+(k+N''-D_j+a) \\
=_{st} \quad & \Pi_{j+1}^+(k-D_j+a+N'+N'') + \Pi_{j+1}^+(k-D_j+a) \\
& - \Pi_{j+1}^+(k-D_j+a+N') - \Pi_{j+1}^+(k-D_j+a+N'') \\
\leq_{st} \quad & 0. \qquad (5.28)
\end{aligned}$$

The last inequality holds, because it reduces to 0 if $(N'=0) \vee (N''=0)$ and it is $\leq_{st} 0$ by induction assumption if $(N'=1) \wedge (N''=1)$.

Case 2. $(a_{j+1}(\mathcal{S}1)=0) \wedge (a_{j+1}(\mathcal{S}2)=1)$. Within case 2, we distinguish two subcases:

Subcase 2a. $(N'=0) \wedge (N''=1)$. In this case, let $\mathcal{S}3$ take the same action at $j+1$ as $\mathcal{S}2$ and $\mathcal{S}4$ the same action as $\mathcal{S}1$. We end up with

$$\begin{aligned}
& \Pi_j^+(k+2) + \Pi_j^+(k) - \Pi_j^+(k+1|a_{j+1}(\mathcal{S}3)=1) \\
& \quad - \Pi_j^+(k+1|a_{j+1}(\mathcal{S}4)=0) \\
=_{st} \quad & \Pi_{j+1}^+(k+N'+N''-D_j) + r_{j+1} + \Pi_{j+1}^+(k-D_j+1) \\
& - r_{j+1} - \Pi_{j+1}^+(k+N'-D_j+1) - \Pi_{j+1}^+(k+N''-D_j) \\
=_{st} \quad & \Pi_{j+1}^+(k+1-D_j) + \Pi_{j+1}^+(k-D_j+1) - \Pi_{j+1}^+(k-D_j+1) \\
& - \Pi_{j+1}^+(k+1-D_j) \\
=_{st} \quad & 0. \qquad (5.29)
\end{aligned}$$

Subcase 2b. $\neg((N'=0) \wedge (N''=1))$. In this case, let $\mathcal{S}3$ take the same action at $j+1$ as $\mathcal{S}1$ and $\mathcal{S}4$ the same action as $\mathcal{S}2$. We end up with

$$\begin{aligned}
& \Pi_j^+(k+2) + \Pi_j^+(k) - \Pi_j^+(k+1|a_{j+1}(\mathcal{S}3)=0) \\
& \quad - \Pi_j^+(k+1|a_{j+1}(\mathcal{S}4)=1) \\
=_{st} \quad & \Pi_{j+1}^+(k+N'+N''-D_j) + r_{j+1} + \Pi_{j+1}^+(k-D_j+1) \\
& -\Pi_{j+1}^+(k+N'-D_j) - r_{j+1} - \Pi_{j+1}^+(k+N''-D_j+1) \\
=_{st} \quad & \Pi_{j+1}^+(k+N'+N''-D_j) + \Pi_{j+1}^+(k-D_j+1) \\
& -\Pi_{j+1}^+(k+N'-D_j) - \Pi_{j+1}^+(k+N''-D_j+1) \\
=_{st} \quad & 0. \qquad (5.30)
\end{aligned}$$

The last equality holds, because either $N''=0$ or $(N'=1)\wedge(N''=1)$ which reduces the term to 0.

The case $(a_{j+1}(\mathcal{S}1)=1)\wedge(a_{j+1}(\mathcal{S}2)=0)$ is not covered, because it can never occur due to $a_{j+1}(\mathcal{S}1)\leq a_{j+1}(\mathcal{S}2)$ by induction assumption. We have shown that $\Pi_j^+(k+2)+\Pi_j^+(k)-\Pi_j^+(k+1|a_{j+1}(\mathcal{S}3))-\Pi_j^+(k+1|a_{j+1}(\mathcal{S}4))\leq_{st} 0$ for some pre-defined actions of $\mathcal{S}3$ and $\mathcal{S}4$. If the random variables are stochastically ordered, their means are ordered as well. The potential suboptimality of these actions ensures

$$E(\Pi_j^+(k+2)) + E(\Pi_j^+(k)) - E(\Pi_j^+(k+1)) - E(\Pi_j^+(k+1)) \leq 0 \qquad (5.31)$$

which completes the proof for any $k=0...c-2$ and any arrival j. The proof is related to the proof of Lemma 2 in Örmeci and Burnetas (2004). ■

Proof of Proposition 5.2. At first, we prove the observation that only events 1 to 3 can occur after accepting a customer. Assume a threshold policy with dynamic threshold level T_j at arrival j. The arrival process is given by $\{(A_j, CL_j)\}$. The system state of the rental system is defined as

$$N_j^- = N_{j-1}^+ - \sum_{i=1}^{N_{j-1}^+} X_{i,j-1} \qquad (5.32)$$

and

$$N_j^+ = \begin{cases} \min\left(c, N_j^- + 1\right) & CL_j = 1 \\ \min(T_j, N_j^- + 1) & CL_j = 2 \end{cases} \tag{5.33}$$

with $X_{i,j}$ as the departure event of customer i in time interval $[A_j, A_{j+1}]$ ($X_{i,j} = 1$ means that customer i has left the system, $X_{i,j} = 0$ means that the customer is still in the system). Now consider the difference in system states between two rental systems, I_j. Let one system ($\overline{N}$) have accepted a customer $j = 0$ and the other one not ($\underline{N}$). Then, $I_0^+ = \overline{N}_0^+ - \underline{N}_0^+ = +1$. For $j > 0$ we get

$$I_j^- = \overline{N}_j^- - \underline{N}_j^- = \begin{cases} I_{j-1}^+ - X_{\overline{N}_{j-1}^+, j-1} & I_{j-1}^+ = +1 \\ 0 & I_{j-1}^+ = 0 \end{cases} \tag{5.34}$$

and

$$\begin{aligned} I_j^+ &= \overline{N}_j^+ - \underline{N}_j^+ \\ &= \begin{cases} \min\left(c, \underline{N}_j^- + I_j^- + 1\right) - \min\left(c, \underline{N}_j^- + 1\right) & CL_j = 1 \\ \min\left(T_j, \underline{N}_j^- + I_j^- + 1\right) - \min\left(c, T_j + 1\right) & CL_j = 2. \end{cases} \end{aligned} \tag{5.35}$$

We make two observations from Eqs. (5.34) and (5.35): (a) $I_j^- \in \{0, +1\}$ and $I_j^+ \in \{0, +1\}$ for all $j = 0, 1, ...$ and (b) the following statements hold$\left(I_j^- = 0\right) \Rightarrow \left(I_j^+ = 0\right)$ and $\left(I_j^+ = 0\right) \Rightarrow \left(I_{j+1}^- = 0\right)$. Therefore, the system states can only differ by one customer and once they become identical, they will remain identical. The events that may lead to identical system states can only be between arrival times with $X_{\overline{N}_{j-1}^+, j-1} = 0$ (this corresponds with event 3) or at arrival times with either an ADI arrival and $\underline{N}_j^- + 1 = c$ (this corresponds with event 1) or a non-ADI arrival and $\underline{N}_j^- + 1 = T_j$ (this corresponds with event 2). Next, we show that with these three events, the optimal decision is given by Eq. (5.2). For an acceptance to be optimal, it must hold that

$$r_j + E(\overline{\Pi}^+) - E(\underline{\Pi}^+) > 0. \tag{5.36}$$

Now consider the difference in the two systems. They accept the same customers until one of the three events is reached and accept the same customers after this event. Thus, we have

$$E(\overline{\Pi}^+) - E(\underline{\Pi}^+) = \Delta\Pi_1^+ P_1(\underline{N}^-, R) + \Delta\Pi_2^+ P_2(\underline{N}^-, R) + \Delta\Pi_3^+ P_3(\underline{N}^-, R). \quad (5.37)$$

Using the $\Delta\Pi_i^+$ from the definition of the events and re-arranging the terms lead to Eq. (5.2), which completes the proof. ■

Proof of Proposition 5.3. The system without ADI is a Markov system. It forms a continuous-time Markov chain with a discrete state space. Due to its irreducibility and its finite state space, it has a unique steady state solution which can be found by solving the global balance equations. The balance equations are given by

$$\begin{aligned} & \pi_k \left(\lambda_I + \lambda_{II} \mathbf{1}\left(k < T\right) + k\right) \\ = \quad & (k+1)\pi_{k+1} + \left(\lambda_I + \lambda_{II} \mathbf{1}\left(k - 1 < T\right)\right) \pi_{k-1}. \end{aligned} \quad (5.38)$$

with π_k as the steady state probability of being in state $k = 0...c-1$. Note that the π_k must sum to 1 with $k = 0...c$. With the steady state probabilities, the service rates $V_I(\Gamma^T)$ and $V_{II}(\Gamma^T)$ are given by

$$V_I(\Gamma^T) = \lambda_I(1 - \pi_c) \quad (5.39)$$

and

$$V_{II}(\Gamma^T) = \lambda_{II}(1 - \sum_{k=T}^{c} \pi_k). \quad (5.40)$$

The profit follows from Eq. (5.1). T^* is the value that maximizes expected profit for given parameters. ■

Proof of Proposition 5.4. We prove that the optimal solution of the program converges towards an upper bound of the optimal profit of our system if $\widehat{t} \to \infty$. Next, we explain why the terminal value of the dynamic programming problem does not affect the average reward per time unit if $\widehat{t} \to \infty$. Our argumentation is as follows: If the inter-arrival time $A_{j+1} - A_j$ between a non-ADI arrival and its successor is large enough, accepting the customer becomes optimal for any system state k. This is the case when $\Pi_j^+(k) - \Pi_j^+(k+1) < r_{II}$ for any $k = 0...c-1$. In an infinitely long sample path such an event occurs with probability 1. Any decision before that event is independent of the terminal value. Since the sample path is infinitely long with $\widehat{t} \to \infty$ and assuming a finite terminal value, the impact of this value on the average reward per time unit vanishes. Thus, if $\widehat{t} \to \infty$ the optimal solution of the stochastic program becomes the optimal solution of a system with infinite time horizon in which all demands are known.

Note that the optimal policy of our ADI system (with ADI demand available only for the next τ time units) is a feasible policy for the case of completely known demand (the system manager could simply ignore some of the demand information). Thus, we have

$$\Pi(\Gamma^*) \leq \lim_{\widehat{t} \to \infty} \frac{\widehat{\Pi}(\widehat{t})}{\widehat{t}}. \tag{5.41}$$

■

Proof of Lemma 5.1. The proof of this lemma proceeds as follows. At first, we split the set of eigenvalues of $\mathbf{Q}$ into two groups. For the first group, we can explicitly determine the eigenvalues in closed-form. It can be seen that the eigenvalues from this group are distinct. For the second group, we show that the eigenvalues are the same eigenvalues as the eigenvalues of a submatrix of $\mathbf{Q}$. We prove that this submatrix is symmetric, which ensures that its eigenvalues are real and distinct. We finalize the proof by showing that, even if some eigenvalues in the first group overlap with eigenvalues in the second group, its corresponding eigenvectors are linearly independent.

We begin by taking a close look at the generator matrix $\mathbf{Q}$. Using the method of determinant expansion in cofactors (cf. Strang (1980), p. 165-167), we can write the determinant of $\mathbf{Q} - w\mathbf{I_c}$ as (let w be a real number and $\mathbf{I_c}$ be the unit matrix corresponding to the dimensions of $\mathbf{Q}$)

$$|\mathbf{Q} - w\mathbf{I_c}| = \sum_{j=0}^{c} (-1)^{j+c} (\mathbf{Q} - w\mathbf{I_c})_{cj} M_{cj} \tag{5.42}$$

where M_{cj} is the determinant of a submatrix of $\mathbf{Q} - w\mathbf{I_c}$ with the last row and the jth column deleted. Since $(\mathbf{Q})_{cj} = 0$ for all j, the determinant reduces to

$$|\mathbf{Q} - w\mathbf{I_c}| = (-1)^{2c}(-w)M_{cc} = -w \left|\widetilde{\mathbf{Q}} - w\mathbf{I_{c-1}}\right| \tag{5.43}$$

with $\widetilde{\mathbf{Q}}$ as the submatrix of $\mathbf{Q}$ with the last row and the last column deleted. We can immediately see that $w = 0$ is an eigenvalue and that all eigenvalues of the reduced matrix $\widetilde{\mathbf{Q}}$ are also eigenvalues of $\mathbf{Q}$. The resulting matrix has only one non-zero entry in the last column, so we can again apply the method of determinant expansion. If $T < c$, we can repeat the same procedure for all columns $j \geq T$ and get

$$|\mathbf{Q} - w\mathbf{I_c}| = -w \left(\prod_{j=T}^{c-1} (-j - w) \right) \left|\widehat{\mathbf{Q}} - w\mathbf{I_T}\right| \tag{5.44}$$

with $\widehat{\mathbf{Q}}$ as a $T \times T$ submatrix of $\mathbf{Q}$ in the upper left corner (i.e., with the first T entries in each dimension). We can see that, $w = 0$, $w = -T, -(T+1), ..., -c+1$, and the T eigenvalues of $\widehat{\mathbf{Q}}$ are the $c+1$ eigenvalues of matrix $\mathbf{Q}$.

For the special case of $T = 0$, the eigenvalues of $\mathbf{Q}$ are $w = 0, -1, ..., -c+1$ with $w = 0$ occurring twice. However, the two eigenvectors resulting from $w = 0$ are linearly independent, as can be seen from the matrix setup: Assume that $\mathbf{u} = (u_0, u_2, ..., u_c)^{\mathbf{T}}$ is an eigenvector of $\mathbf{Q}$ corresponding to $w = 0$. Then, we have $u_0 = u_1 = u_2 = ... = u_{c-1}$ so that u_{c-1} and u_c can be chosen arbitrarily. We can construct two linearly independent eigenvectors.

For $T > 0$ we have to analyze the eigenvalues of $\widehat{\mathbf{Q}}$, which we do next. Let $\mathbf{A}$

be a diagonal $T \times T$ matrix with diagonal element $(\mathbf{A})_{ii} = \sqrt{\frac{\lambda_{II}^i}{i!}}$. Then, we have

$$\begin{aligned}\left(\mathbf{A}\widehat{\mathbf{Q}}\mathbf{A}^{-1}\right)_{ij} &= \sum_{k=0}^{T-1} (\mathbf{A})_{ik} \left(\widehat{\mathbf{Q}}\mathbf{A}^{-1}\right)_{kj} = \sum_{k=0}^{T-1} (\mathbf{A})_{ik} \sum_{n=0}^{T-1} \left(\widehat{\mathbf{Q}}\right)_{kn} (\mathbf{A}^{-1})_{nj} \\ &= (\mathbf{A})_{ii} \left(\widehat{\mathbf{Q}}\right)_{ij} (\mathbf{A}^{-1})_{jj} = \sqrt{\frac{\lambda_{II}^i}{i!} \frac{j!}{\lambda_{II}^j}} \left(\widehat{\mathbf{Q}}\right)_{ij}. \qquad (5.45)\end{aligned}$$

It follows that matrix $\mathbf{A}\widehat{\mathbf{Q}}\mathbf{A}^{-1}$ is symmetric, because the only non-zero, off-diagonal entries of $\widehat{\mathbf{Q}}$ are $\left(\widehat{\mathbf{Q}}\right)_{i,i-1} = i$ and $\left(\widehat{\mathbf{Q}}\right)_{i,i+1} = \lambda_{II}$, and so the following equation holds

$$\begin{aligned}\left(\mathbf{A}\widehat{\mathbf{Q}}\mathbf{A}^{-1}\right)_{i,i-1} &= \sqrt{\frac{\lambda_{II}^i}{i!} \frac{(i-1)!}{\lambda_{II}^{i-1}}} \left(\widehat{\mathbf{Q}}\right)_{i,i-1} \\ &= \sqrt{\frac{\lambda_{II}}{i}} \left(\widehat{\mathbf{Q}}\right)_{i,i-1} = \sqrt{\lambda_{II} i} = \lambda_{II} \sqrt{\frac{i}{\lambda_{II}}} \\ &= \sqrt{\frac{\lambda_{II}^{i-1}}{(i-1)!} \frac{i!}{\lambda_{II}^i}} \left(\widehat{\mathbf{Q}}\right)_{i-1,i} = \left(\mathbf{A}\widehat{\mathbf{Q}}\mathbf{A}^{-1}\right)_{i-1,i}. \qquad (5.46)\end{aligned}$$

The symmetric matrix $\mathbf{A}\widehat{\mathbf{Q}}\mathbf{A}^{-1}$ corresponds with an undirected graph whose T vertices are connected in one line (because its only non-zero entries are located in the diagonal, the sub-diagonal, and the super-diagonal). Thus, the graph complies with the definition of a tree. Leal-Duarte and Johnson (2002) have shown that symmetric matrices whose graphs form trees have at least as many distinct eigenvalues as vertices in the longest path of the tree. It follows that matrix $\mathbf{A}\widehat{\mathbf{Q}}\mathbf{A}^{-1}$ has at least T distinct eigenvalues. Since it can have at most T eigenvalues, we conclude that all eigenvalues of matrix $\mathbf{A}\widehat{\mathbf{Q}}\mathbf{A}^{-1}$ are distinct. They are also real, because symmetric matrices always have real eigenvalues (cf. Strang (1980), p. 222-224). Matrix $\mathbf{A}\widehat{\mathbf{Q}}\mathbf{A}^{-1}$ is similar to $\widehat{\mathbf{Q}}$, so $\widehat{\mathbf{Q}}$ has the same real and distinct eigenvalues. Eigenvectors of distinct eigenvalues are always linearly independent (cf. Strang (1980), p. 192). Note that the eigenvalues of $\widehat{\mathbf{Q}}$ are also non-zero due to the following argumentation: $\widehat{\mathbf{Q}}$ differs from the generator matrix $\mathbf{Q}_{Erlang}$ of an

Erlang Loss system with $T-1$ servers, arrival rate λ_{II} and departure rate 1 only by the last entry, $\left(\widehat{\mathbf{Q}}\right)_{T-1T-1} = 1-\lambda_{II}-T \neq 1-T = \left(\mathbf{Q}_{Erlang}\right)_{T-1T-1}$. Because $\mathbf{Q}_{Erlang}$ has a steady state solution, $\boldsymbol{\pi}\mathbf{Q}_{Erlang} = \overline{\mathbf{0}}$ holds for a certain row vector $\boldsymbol{\pi} = (\pi_0, ..., \pi_{T-1})$ with all $\pi_i > 0$. Then, we see by equating the last columns of matrices $\widehat{\mathbf{Q}}$ and $\mathbf{Q}_{Erlang}$ that $\boldsymbol{\pi}\widehat{\mathbf{Q}} = \overline{\mathbf{0}}$ could only hold if

$$T-1 = \lambda_{II} + T - 1, \tag{5.47}$$

which is not possible due to $\lambda_{II} > 0$. Thus, $w = 0$ cannot be an eigenvalue of $\widehat{\mathbf{Q}}$.

Next, we show that even if some eigenvalues of $\widehat{\mathbf{Q}}$ overlap with the eigenvalues $w = -T, -(T+1), ..., -c+1$, the corresponding eigenvectors are linearly independent so that the algebraic multiplicity and the geometric multiplicity of these eigenvalues coincide. We do this by showing that, if $w \in \{-T, -(T+1), ..., -c+1\}$ is also an eigenvalue of $\widehat{\mathbf{Q}}$, $\mathbf{Q}$ has two linearly independent eigenvectors $\widetilde{u}$ and $\widetilde{v}$ corresponding to w.

Let $\mathbf{B}$ be a submatrix of $\mathbf{Q}$ from the lower right corner except the last row and column, i.e., $\mathbf{B}$ looks like

$$\mathbf{B} = \begin{pmatrix} -T & 0 & 0 & 0 \\ T+1 & -T-1 & 0 & 0 \\ \cdots & \cdots & \cdots & 0 \\ 0 & 0 & c-1 & -c+1 \end{pmatrix}. \tag{5.48}$$

Clearly, w is an eigenvalue of $\mathbf{B}$, because of $w \in \{-T, -(T+1), ..., -c+1\}$. Assume that vector $\mathbf{u}$ is an eigenvector of $\mathbf{B}$ that corresponds to w. Then, vector $\widetilde{\mathbf{u}} = \begin{pmatrix} \overline{\mathbf{0}} \\ \mathbf{u} \\ 0 \end{pmatrix} \in \mathbb{R}^{c+1}$ is an eigenvector of $\mathbf{Q}$, because from $\mathbf{B}\mathbf{u} = w\mathbf{u}$ follows $\mathbf{Q}\widetilde{\mathbf{u}} = w\widetilde{\mathbf{u}}$.

Now, assume that $\mathbf{v} = (v_0, v_1, ..., v_{T-1})^{\mathbf{T}}$ is an eigenvector of submatrix $\widehat{\mathbf{Q}}$ corresponding to the eigenvalue w so that $\widehat{\mathbf{Q}}\mathbf{v} = w\mathbf{v}$. The eigenvector of the complete matrix $\mathbf{Q}$ looks like $\widetilde{\mathbf{v}} = \begin{pmatrix} \mathbf{v} \\ \mathbf{x} \\ 0 \end{pmatrix} \in \mathbb{R}^{c+1}$ with $\mathbf{x} \in \mathbb{R}^{c-T}$ such that condition $\mathbf{Q}\widetilde{\mathbf{v}} = w\widetilde{\mathbf{v}}$ is met. The components x_i of $\mathbf{x}$ exist, because there must be a vector $\widetilde{\mathbf{v}}$ that satisfies $\mathbf{Q}\widetilde{\mathbf{v}} = w\widetilde{\mathbf{v}}$, and they can be derived recursively.

As we have shown, vectors $\widetilde{\mathbf{u}}$ and $\widetilde{\mathbf{v}}$ are eigenvectors of $\mathbf{Q}$ corresponding to eigenvalue w. Note that each of the subvectors $\mathbf{u}$ and $\mathbf{v}$ has at least one non-zero component, because both are eigenvectors by themselves. Then, vectors $\widetilde{\mathbf{u}}$ and $\widetilde{\mathbf{v}}$ are linearly independent, because

$$\alpha_1\widetilde{\mathbf{u}} + \alpha_2\widetilde{\mathbf{v}} = \overline{\mathbf{0}} \Leftrightarrow \begin{pmatrix} \overline{\mathbf{0}} + \alpha_2\mathbf{v} \\ \alpha_1\mathbf{u} + \alpha_2\mathbf{x} \\ 0 \end{pmatrix} = \begin{pmatrix} \overline{\mathbf{0}} \\ \overline{\mathbf{0}} \\ 0 \end{pmatrix} \tag{5.49}$$

can hold only if $\alpha_1 = \alpha_2 = 0$. Scalar α_2 must be zero to have $\alpha_2\mathbf{v} = \overline{\mathbf{0}}$ and this also requires $\alpha_1 = 0$ in order to have $\alpha_1\mathbf{u} + 0\mathbf{x} = \overline{\mathbf{0}}$.

We have shown that all eigenvalues of $\mathbf{Q}$ are real and that there can be at most pairwise identical eigenvalues. For these eigenvalues, the eigenvectors must be linearly independent. Thus, all eigenvectors of $\mathbf{Q}$ are linearly independent. This ensures diagonalizability (cf. Strang (1980), p. 190). ■

Proof of Lemma 5.2. We proceed by calculating the probabilities of each path in the probability tree given in Figure 5.2. The probability of event $S \leq A_n - A_{n-1}$ is conveniently given by $F_S(A_n - A_{n-1}) = 1 - e^{-(A_n - A_{n-1})}$. The probability that the CTMC is in state j at the end of the interval, $P(N^- = j)$, is given by $\left(\boldsymbol{\pi}_n^-\right)_j$. The cdf of the first passage time of the system into state c, $T_{\cdot c}$, given the initial distribution $\boldsymbol{\pi}_{n-1}^+$, is

$$\begin{aligned} P\left(T_{\cdot c} \leq t\right) &= \left(\boldsymbol{\pi}_{n-1}^+\right)\left(\mathbf{P}(t)\right)_c = \left(\boldsymbol{\pi}_{n-1}^+\right)\left(\mathbf{U}\mathbf{D}(t)\mathbf{U}^{-1}\right)_c \\ &= \sum_{k=0}^{c} e^{w_k t} \sum_{i=0}^{c} \left(\boldsymbol{\pi}_{n-1}^+\right)_i \mathbf{U}_{ik}\mathbf{U}_{kc}^{-1}. \end{aligned} \tag{5.50}$$

Note that Equation (5.50) holds because state c is absorbing. We begin by determining p_{3n}. We have that

$$\begin{aligned}
p_{3n} &= P(S \leq A_n - A_{n-1} \wedge N^- < c) \\
&\quad + P(S \leq A_n - A_{n-1} \wedge N^- = c \wedge S \leq T_{\cdot c}) \\
&= P(S \leq T_{\cdot c} \wedge S \leq A_n - A_{n-1}) \\
&= P(S \leq \min(T_{\cdot c}, A_n - A_{n-1})) \\
&= \int_0^{+\infty} P(S = t)\left[1 - P(\min(T_{\cdot c}, A_n - A_{n-1}) \leq t)\right] dt \\
&= \int_0^{+\infty} e^{-t} dt - \int_0^{A_n - A_{n-1}} e^{-t} P(T_{\cdot c} \leq t) dt \\
&\quad - \int_{A_n - A_{n-1}}^{+\infty} e^{-t} P(A_n - A_{n-1} \leq t) dt \\
&= 1 - \int_{A_n - A_{n-1}}^{+\infty} e^{-t} dt - \int_0^{A_n - A_{n-1}} e^{-t} P(T_{\cdot c} \leq t) dt \\
&= 1 - e^{-(A_n - A_{n-1})} - \int_0^{A_n - A_{n-1}} \sum_{k=0}^{c} e^{-t} e^{w_k t} \sum_{i=0}^{c} \left(\boldsymbol{\pi}_{n-1}^{+}\right)_i \mathbf{U}_{ik} \mathbf{U}_{kc}^{-1} dt \\
&= 1 - e^{-(A_n - A_{n-1})} \\
&\quad - \sum_{k=0}^{c} \left(\sum_{i=0}^{c} \left(\boldsymbol{\pi}_{n-1}^{+}\right)_i \mathbf{U}_{ik} \mathbf{U}_{kc}^{-1} \right) \int_0^{A_n - A_{n-1}} e^{(w_k - 1)t} dt \\
&= 1 - e^{-(A_n - A_{n-1})} \\
&\quad - \sum_{k=0}^{c} \left(\sum_{i=0}^{c} \left(\boldsymbol{\pi}_{n-1}^{+}\right)_i \mathbf{U}_{ik} \mathbf{U}_{kc}^{-1} \right) \alpha_k (A_n - A_{n-1}) \qquad (5.51)
\end{aligned}$$

and

$$\alpha_k(x) = \int_0^x e^{(w_k - 1)t} dt = \begin{cases} \frac{\left(e^{(w_k - 1)x} - 1\right)}{w_k - 1} & w_k \neq 1 \\ x & w_k = 1 \end{cases} . \qquad (5.52)$$

Likewise, the probability of event 2 occurring first, p_{2n}, is given by

$$\begin{aligned}
p_{2n} &= P(S > A_n - A_{n-1} \wedge N^- = c) \\
&\quad + P(S \leq A_n - A_{n-1} \wedge N^- = c \wedge S > T_{\cdot c}) \\
&= P(S > A_n - A_{n-1} \wedge N^- = c \wedge S > T_{\cdot c}) \\
&\quad + P(S \leq A_n - A_{n-1} \wedge N^- = c \wedge S > T_{\cdot c}) \\
&= P(N^- = c \wedge S > T_{\cdot c}) \\
&= P(T_{\cdot c} \leq A_n - A_{n-1} \wedge T_{\cdot c} \leq S) \\
&= P(T_{\cdot c} \leq \min(S, A_n - A_{n-1})) \\
&= \int_0^{+\infty} P(T_{\cdot c} \leq \min(t, A_n - A_{n-1}))P(S = t)dt \\
&= \int_0^{A_n - A_{n-1}} P(T_{\cdot c} \leq t)e^{-t}dt + \int_{A_n - A_{n-1}}^{+\infty} P(T_{\cdot c} \leq A_n - A_{n-1})e^{-t}dt \\
&= \sum_{k=0}^{c} \left(\sum_{i=0}^{c} \left(\boldsymbol{\pi}_{n-1}^{+}\right)_i \mathbf{U}_{ik} \mathbf{U}_{kc}^{-1} \right) \alpha_k(A_n - A_{n-1}) \\
&\quad + \left(\boldsymbol{\pi}_n^{-}\right)_c e^{-(A_n - A_{n-1})}.
\end{aligned} \tag{5.53}$$

The probability of event 1 is easier to compute with

$$\begin{aligned}
p_{1n} &= P\left(S > A_n - A_{n-1} \wedge N^- = c - 1\right) \\
&= P\left(S > A_n - A_{n-1}\right) P\left(N^- = c - 1\right) \\
&= e^{-(A_n - A_{n-1})} \left(\boldsymbol{\pi}_n^{-}\right)_{c-1},
\end{aligned} \tag{5.54}$$

because the two random variables S and N^- are independent. ■

Proof of Proposition 5.5. The proof is straightforward and proceeds by induction. Start with the first decision for arrival $j = 0$. Define a policy $\widehat{\Gamma}_0$ which uses the decision logic of the ADI policy for arrival $j = 0$ and the decision logic of the optimal state-dependent threshold policy Γ^T for all future admission decisions.

In this case, the computation of the event probabilities p_{10}, p_{20}, and p_{30} is exact, because the ADI policy also assumes a state-dependent threshold policy for future decisions. For this policy, it holds that

$$\Pi\left(\widehat{\Gamma}_0\right) \geq \Pi\left(\Gamma^T\right), \tag{5.55}$$

because the decision of $\widehat{\Gamma}_0$ for $j = 0$ is optimal, i.e.,

$$\Pi\left(\widehat{\Gamma}_0\right) = \max(r_0 + \Pi_0^+(k+1), \Pi_0^+(k)) \geq \Pi\left(\Gamma^T\right). \tag{5.56}$$

Assume a policy $\widehat{\Gamma}_{j-1}$, which admits all customers after $j-1$ with a state-dependent threshold policy. Then, we can define a policy $\widehat{\Gamma}_j$ for non-ADI arrival j, which takes the same decision as $\widehat{\Gamma}_{j-1}$ up to arrival $j-1$, decides with the decision logic of the ADI policy for arrival j and behaves like a state-dependent threshold policy Γ^T for all future arrivals.

Then, we have

$$\begin{aligned} \Pi\left(\widehat{\Gamma}_j\right) &= \sum_{k=0}^{j-1} r_k a_k + \max(r_j + \Pi_j^+(k+1), \Pi_j^+(k)) \\ &\geq \sum_{k=0}^{j-1} r_k a_k + r_j a'_j + \Pi_j^+(k + a'_j) = \Pi\left(\widehat{\Gamma}_{j-1}\right). \end{aligned} \tag{5.57}$$

for an arbitrary decision a'_j of policy $\widehat{\Gamma}_{j-1}$. Note that the two policies differ only in the decision for arrival j. Assume that $\Pi\left(\widehat{\Gamma}_{j-1}\right) \geq \Pi\left(\Gamma^T\right)$ holds (which we have shown for $j-1=0$). From Equation (5.57) follows by induction that

$$\Pi\left(\widehat{\Gamma}_j\right) \geq \Pi\left(\widehat{\Gamma}_{j-1}\right) \geq \Pi\left(\Gamma^T\right) \tag{5.58}$$

for all $j = 0, 1, 2, ...$, even when $j \to +\infty$. It is obvious that

$$\Pi\left(\Gamma^{ADI}\right) = \lim_{j\to\infty} \Pi\left(\widehat{\Gamma}_j\right) \geq \Pi\left(\Gamma^T\right), \tag{5.59}$$

because we replace all decisions of policy Γ^T by the decisions of policy Γ^{ADI}. ■

Chapter 6

Conclusion

In this thesis, we presented models of B2B vehicle rental systems and we showed how to analyze and optimize these models. The models and their analyses were given in the four main chapters. Each chapter represented a mostly independent piece of research. Next, we summarize the main results of each chapter. Then, we critically review our way of modeling rental systems. Finally, we provide an outlook into further research.

Summary of Key Results In Chapter 2, we analyzed a stochastic rental model with batch arrivals and with identical rental times within customer orders. We allowed for seasonality in the demand and the rental times of the customers. For this model, we showed how to optimize the fleet size such that expected profit is maximized. Because the implementation of the optimization procedure is complex, we described an approximation formula that is very easy to calculate. We also showed how the rental company can optimally employ leased cars during periods of peak demand and how leasing affects the optimal fleet size of owned cars. For the case of multiple fleets with similar cars, we derived conditions under which merging these fleets is beneficial. We supported our analysis by numerical experiments from real data of the company that motivated our research. We performed the experiments twice, one time with our analytical model and one time with a detailed simulation model that was built to simulate the rail car operations at this

F. Papier, *Optimization of Rental Systems*, Edition KWV,
https://doi.org/10.1007/978-3-658-24313-5_6

company. A comparison of the experimental results revealed that our analytical models performs close to the simulation model and, thus, that our analytical model is accurate for fleet planning. We also reported on how our analytical model is implemented at the rail cargo company and how the company uses it to support fleet planning.

In Chapter 3, we considered a very general stochastic rental model. We allowed for arbitrary demand processes and an arbitrary rental time distribution. We further assumed PBB and that rental times are independent between orders but may have an arbitrary dependence within orders. Firstly, we analyzed a model with homogeneous cars and found out that the loss probability is convex in the fleet size, i.e., that the service level is concave in the fleet size. Then, we extended the model to allow for heterogeneous cars that are stochastically ordered from fast to slow. We extended the convexity result of the loss probability to this more general model. Finally, we showed that the same models under EBB do not necessarily have convex loss probabilities and that the intuitive idea of ordering servers from fast to slow does not necessarily lead to minimal loss probabilities.

In Chapter 4, we analyzed a rental model with two customer classes. One class pays a higher price for the rental service than the other class in order to obtain a service guarantee. We analyzed the model and showed how to find the optimal fleet size and the optimal admission policy to allocate cars to customers. We provided an easy-to-implement algorithm to find the optimal values. We also performed numerical experiments to analyze the effect of system parameters such as mean sizes of customer orders or fleet holding costs on the expected profit, the optimal fleet size, and the optimal rationing level. We found that batching customer orders has a substantial effect on the optimal expected profit and the optimal fleet size. We also derived conditions under which using rationing is especially worthwhile.

In Chapter 5, we analyzed a rental model with two customer classes under advance demand information. As in the previous chapter, we assumed that one customer class pays a higher price for the rental service than the other class to receive a service guarantee. In addition, we assumed that this high-priority customer class provides its demand information a certain time in advance, and we employed these additional information to improve the admission policy. We showed that the optimal admission policy is of threshold type, i.e., that rationing low-priority customer demand is optimal. However, computing the optimal threshold level turned out to be computationally intractable. Therefore, we developed a heuristic policy that makes use of ADI. For this policy, we could analytically show that it always outperforms policies that do not take into account ADI. We also performed numerical experiments with data from the rail cargo company. The results showed that the potential of using ADI can be substantial in rental systems and that our heuristic policy performs close to optimal.

Critical Review of Modeling Framework In all four main chapters in this thesis, we used a common framework for modeling rental systems. While this way of modeling proved very effective in terms of accuracy and richness of the results, it is not necessarily the only way to model rental systems and it certainly has its drawbacks.

A major characteristic of our rental models is that we do not explicitly model the operations that take place during the rental time. We model these operations only through the total rental time, because we are only interested in the effect that the operations have on the availability of the cars. Our approach enabled us to analytically derive structural results of the rental models. We could make this assumption, because in the scenarios that we considered, the transportation time was only a minor part of the total rental time and, therefore, the transportation network with its different locations had only a negligible impact on the planning problem. In Section 2.7, we verified the accuracy of our approach for the rental systems at the company that motivated our research. However, in systems where the transportation time represents a large part of the total rental time, the spatial transportation network might have a significant impact on the planning problem so that our assumption could not be made.

For the rental models analyzed, we showed how to find the optimal fleet size, the optimal fleet structure, and the optimal admission policy. However, this is not enough to operate vehicle rental systems. Day-to-day operational planning is necessary to distribute empty vehicles over the region the company operates in. For this task, further operational models are required to support decision making, and these models have to fit to the planning models in this thesis.

Outlook into Further Research In the main chapters of this thesis, we hinted at possible further extensions of our models. Now, we highlight two main directions for further research that seem to be particularly promising.

One way to extend our results would be to focus on the effect that large-scale incidents, such as the introduction of a new fleet or a sudden slump in demand, have on the performance of a rental system. It would be interesting to see how long it takes the system to return to normal behavior and how profit is affected during this time.

Another way to extend our research is to keep pace with the new service and pricing models that are currently emerging in the cargo logistics industry. For example, pricing rental services has recently gained increasing attention. Integrating pricing decisions with operational fleet planning issues is a topic that is likely to support decision makers in the cargo logistics industry and that fits well into current research.

While we are convinced that this thesis is a significant contribution to the known research on fleet planning in rental systems, we are aware that many questions remain for further research on this topic.

Bibliography

Albright, S.C. 1977. Structure of optimal policies in complex queueing systems. *Operations Research* **25** 1020-1027.

Alnowibet, K., H. Perros. 2006. The nonstationary loss queue: A survey. J. Barria, ed. *Communication Networks and Computer Systems.* Imperial College Press, London.

Altman, E., T. Jimenez, G. Koole. 2001. On optimal call admission control in a resource-sharing system. *IEEE Transactions on Communications* **49** 1659-1668.

Baker, K., M. Magazine, H. Nuttle. 1986. The effect of commonality on safety stock in a simple inventory model. *Management Science* **32** 982-988.

Barnhart, C., G. Laporte. 2007. *Handbooks in operations research and management science Vol. 14 - Transportation.* North-Holland, Amsterdam.

Beaujon, G., M. Turnquist. 1991. A model for fleet sizing and vehicle allocation. *Transportation Science* **25** 19-45.

Bojovic, N. 2002. A general system theory approach to rail freight car fleet sizing. *European Journal of Operational Research* **136** 136-172.

BRS (Barry, Rogliano & Salles). 2006. *Alphaliner Report 2006.* Paris.

Carrizosa, E., E. Conde, M. Munoz-Marquez. 1998. Admission policies in loss queueing models with heterogeneous arrivals. *Management Science* **44** 311-320.

F. Papier, *Optimization of Rental Systems*, Edition KWV,
https://doi.org/10.1007/978-3-658-24313-5

Cooper, R.B., P. Palakurthi. 1989. Heterogeneous-Server loss systems with ordered entry: An anomaly. *Operations Research Letters* **8** 347–349.

Crainic, T., G. Laporte. 1998. *Fleet management and logistics.* Kluwer Academic Publishers, Boston.

DataMonitor. 2003. Road & rail in Europe - Industry profile. *DataMonitor Industry Profiles.*

DataMonitor. 2005. Road & rail in Europe - Industry profile. *DataMonitor Industry Profiles.*

DataMonitor. 2006. Truck rental in Europe - Industry profile. *DataMonitor Industry Profiles.*

DataMonitor. 2007. Global transportation - Industry profile. *DataMonitor Industry Profiles.*

Deshpande, V., M.A. Cohen, K. Donohue. 2003. A threshold inventory rationing policy for service-differentiated demand classes. *Management Science* **49** 683-703.

Du, Y., R. Hall. 1997. Fleet sizing and empty equipment redistribution for center-terminal transportation networks. *Management Science* **43** 145-157.

Economou, A., A. Fakinos. 1999. Product form stationary distributions for the $M/G/k$ group-arrival, group-departure loss system under a general acceptance policy. *European Journal of Operational Research* **112** 196–206.

Erlang, A.K. 1918. Solutions of some problems in the theory of probabilities of significance in automatic telephone exchanges. *The Post Office Electrical Engineers Journal* **10** 189-197.

European Commission. 2007. *Transport - Rail transport & interoperability.* URL: ec.europa.eu/transport/rail/market/freight_en.htm, 9.9.2007.

European Communities. 2006. Eurostat database - Industry, trade and services.

European Rental Association. 2007. *Why rent?* URL: www.erarental.org/whyrent.asp, 8.9.2007.

Fakinos, D., K. Sirakoulis. 1989. Product-Form distributions for an M/G/k group-arrival group-departure loss system. *Advances in Applied Probability* **21** 721-724.

Feller, W. 1971. *An Introduction to Probability Theory and Its Applications - Volume II.* John Wiley & Sons, New York.

Ferrulli, G. 2007. Can carriers solve their dilemma? *The Journal of Commerce* **8** 37.

Frank, K.C., R.Q. Zhang, I. Duenyas. 2003. Optimal policies for inventory systems with priority demand classes. *Operations Research* **51** 993-1002.

Frantzeskakis, L., W. Powell. 1990. A successive linear approximation procedure for stochastic, dynamic vehicle allocation problems. *Transportation Science* **24** 40-57.

Fulkerson, D. 1961. An out-of-kilter method for minimal-cost flow problems. *Journal of the Society for Industrial and Applied Mathematics* **9** 18-27.

Gallego, G., Ö. Özer. 2001. Integrating replenishment decisions with advance demand information. *Management Science* **47** 1344–1360.

Gallego, G., Ö. Özer. 2003. Optimal replenishment policies for multi-echelon inventory problems under advance demand information. *Manufacturing & Service Operations Management* **5** 157-175.

Gans, N., S. Savin. 2007. Pricing and capacity rationing in rentals with uncertain durations. *Management Science* **53** 390-407.

Gerchak, Y., D. Mossman. 1992. On the effect of demand randomness on inventories and costs. *Operations Research* **40** 804-807.

Godfrey, G., W. Powell. 2002a. An adaptive dynamic programming algorithm for dynamic fleet management, I: single period travel times. *Transportation Science* **36** 21-39.

Godfrey, G., W. Powell. 2002b. An adaptive dynamic programming algorithm for dynamic fleet management, II: multiperiod travel times. *Transportation Science* **36** 40-54.

Ha, A. 1997. Inventory rationing in a make-to-stock production system with several demand classes and lost sales. *Management Science* **43** 1093-1103.

Ha, A. 2000. Stock rationing in a $M/E_k/1$ make-to-stock queue. *Management Science* **46** 77-87.

Hariharan, R., P. Zipkin. 1995. Customer order information, lead times, and inventories. *Management Science* **41** 1599–1607.

IICL (Institute of International Container Lessors). 2006. *Annual Leased Container Fleet Survey - 2006.* New York.

Iravani, S., T.M. Liu, K.L. Luangkesorn, D. Simchi-Levi. 2007. A produce-to-stock system with advance demand information and secondary customers. *Naval Research Logistics* **54** 331-345.

Jordan, W., M. Turnquist. 1983. A stochastic network model for railroad car distribution. *Transportation Science* **17** 123-145.

Kawanishi, K., Y. Takahashi, T. Takenaka. 2000. Trunk reservation effects on multi-server system with batch arrivals of loss and delay customers. *IEICE Transactions on Communications* **E83-B** 20-29.

Kemeny, J.G., J.L. Snell. 1960. *Finite Markov Chains.* Van Nostrand, Princeton, New Jersey.

King, G., H. Topaloglu. 2006. Incorporating the pricing decisions into the dynamic fleet management problem. Working Paper, Cornell University, New York, United States.

Koenigsberg, E., R. Lam. 1976. Cyclic queue models of fleet operations. *Operations Research* **24** 516–529.

Krummheuer, E. 2007. Waggonvermietung boomt (in German). *Handelsblatt* **158** 14.

Ku, C.-Y., S. Jordan. 1997. Access control to two multiserver loss queues in series. *IEEE Transactions on Automatic Control* **42** 1017-1023.

Ku, C.-Y., S. Jordan. 2002. Access control of parallel multiserver loss queues. *Performance Evaluation* **50** 219-231.

Ku, C.-Y., D. Yen, I.-C. Chang, S.-M. Huang, S. Jordan. 2006. Near-Optimal control policy for loss networks. *Omega* **34** 406-416.

Leal-Duarte, A., C. Johnson. 2002. On the minimum number of distinct eigenvalues for a symmetric matrix whose graph is a given tree. *Mathematical Inequalities and Applications* **5** 175-180.

Lee, H. 1996. Effective inventory and service management through product and process redesign. *Operations Research* **44** 151-159.

Lippman, S.A. 1975. Applying a new device in the optimization of exponential queuing systems. *Operations Research* **23** 687-710.

List, G.F., B. Wood, L.K. Nozick, M.A. Turnquist, D.A. Jones, E.A. Kjeldgaard, C.R. Lawton. 2003. Robust optimization for fleet planning under uncertainty. *Transportation Research, Part E* **39** 209-227.

Liyanage, J., J.G. Shanthikumar. 1992. Second-Order properties of single-stage queueing systems, in: U.N. Bhat, I.V. Basawa. *Queueing and related models.* Clarendon Press, Oxford, England.

Marklund, J. 2006. Controlling inventories in divergent supply chains with advance-order information. *Operations Research* **54** 988-1010.

Messerli, E.J. 1972. Proof of a convexity property of the Erlang B formula. *Bell System Technical Journal* **51** 951–953.

Miller, B. 1969. A queueing reward system with several customer classes. *Management Science* **16** 234-245.

Moehle, M. 2005. Convergence results for compound Poisson distributions and applications to the standard Luria-Delbrueck distribution. *Journal of Applied Probability* **42** 620-631.

Nahmias, S., S.W. Demmy. 1981. Operating characteristics of an inventory system with rationing. *Management Science* **27** 1236-1245.

Nievergelt, E., O. Mueller, F. Schlaepfer, W. Landis. 1970. *Praktische Studien zur Unternehmensforschung (in German).* Springer, Berlin.

Örmeci, E.L., A. Burnetas. 2004. Admission control with batch arrivals. *Operations Research Letters* **32** 448-454.

Örmeci, E., A. Burnetas. 2005. Dynamic admission control for loss systems with batch arrivals. *Advances in Applied Probability* **37** 915-937.

Örmeci, E.L., J. Van Der Wal. 2006. Admission policies for a two class loss system with general interarrival times. *Stochastic Models* **22** 37-53.

Özer, Ö., W. Wei. 2004. Inventory control with limited capacity and advance demand information. *Operations Research* **52** 988-1000.

Papier, F., R.W. Wolff, U. Thonemann. 2007. On the convexity of loss probabilities when arrivals occur in batches and servers are heterogeneous. *Operations Research Letters* **35** 467-471.

Parikh, S. 1977. On a fleet sizing and allocation problem. *Management Science* **23** 972–977.

Powell, W. 1986. A stochastic model of the dynamic vehicle allocation problem. *Transportation Science* **20** 117-129.

Powell, W., T. Carvalho, G. Godfrey, H. Simao. 1995. Dynamic fleet management as a logistics queueing network. *Annals of Operations Research* **61** 165-188.

Powell, W., T. Carvalho. 1998. Dynamic control of logistics queueing networks for large-scale fleet management. *Transportation Science* **32** 90-109.

Ross, K., D. Tsang. 1989. The stochastic knapsack problem. *IEEE Transactions on Communications* **37** 740-747.

Savin, S., M. Cohen, N. Gans, Z. Katalan. 2005. Capacity management in rental businesses with two customer bases. *Operations Research* **53** 617-631.

Sea Containers Ltd. 2005. *Annual Report 2004*. London.

Shanthikumar, J.G., D.D. Yao. 1987. Comparing ordered-entry queues with heterogeneous servers. *Queueing Systems* **2** 235–244.

Sherali, H., C. Tuncbilek. 1997. Static and dynamic time-space strategic models and algorithms for multilevel rail-car fleet management. *Management Science* **43** 235-250.

Shonick, W., J. Jackson. 1973. An improved stochastic model for occupancy-related random variables in general-acute hospitals. *Operations Research* **21** 952-965.

Smith, D. R., W. Whitt. 1981. Resource sharing for efficiency in traffic systems. *The Bell System Technical Journal* **60** 39-55.

Strang, G. 1980. *Linear algebra and its applications (2ed)*. Academic Press, New York.

Tainiter, M. 1964. Some stochastic inventory models for rental situations. *Management Science* **11** 316-326.

Tempelmeier, H. 2006. Supply chain inventory optimization with two customer classes in discrete time. *European Journal of Operational Research* **174** 600-621.

Topaloglu, H., W. Powell. 2006. Dynamic programming approximations for stochastic time-staged integer multicommodity-flow problems. *INFORMS Journal on Computing* **18** 31-42.

Topkis, D. 1968. Optimal ordering and rationing policies in a nonstationary dynamic inventory model with n demand classes. *Management Science* **15** 160-176.

Turnquist, M., W. Jordan. 1986. Fleet sizing under production cycles and uncertain travel times. *Transportation Science* **20** 227–236.

UNCTAD (United Nations Conference on Trade and Development). 1999. *Review of Maritime Tranport 1999.* United Nations, New York and Geneva.

U.S. Census Bureau. 2005. Industry series reports of the year 2002.

Van Looy, B., P. Gemmel, R. Van Dierndonck. 2003. *Services management: An integrated approach (2ed).* Financial Times Prentice-Hall, Harlow, Great Britain.

VTG AG. 2007. *Wertpapierprospekt Juni 2007 (in German).* Hamburg.

Wang, B., S. Savin. 2006. Capacity management in rental businesses with reservations. Working paper, Columbia University, New York, United States.

Weyers, A. 2007. Gueterwagenmanagement (in German). Ph.D. Dissertation, Department of Supply Chain Management and Management Science, University of Cologne, Germany.

Whitt, W. 1984. Heavy-Traffic approximations for service systems with blocking. *AT&T Bell Laboratories Technical Journal* **63** 689-708.

Whitt, W. 1991. The pointwise stationary approximation for Mt/Mt/s queues is asymptotically correct as the rates increase. *Management Science* **37** 307-314.

Wolff, R.W. 1989. *Stochastic modeling and the theory of queues.* Prentice-Hall, Upper Saddle River, New Jersey.

Wolff, R.W., C.-L. Wang. 2002. On the convexity of loss probabilities. *Journal of Applied Probability* **39** 402–406.

Wu, P., J. Hartman, G. Wilson. 2005. An integrated model and solution approach for fleet sizing with heterogeneous assets. *Transportation Science* **39** 87-103.

Yao, D.D. 1986. Convexity properties of the overflow in an ordered-entry system with heterogeneous servers. *Operations Research Letters* **5** 145–147.

Yao, D.D. 1987. The arrangement of servers in an ordered-entry system. *Operations Research* **35** 759–763.

Zhao, H., V. Deshpande, J.K. Ryan. 2005. Inventory sharing and rationing in decentralized dealer networks. *Management Science* **51** 531-547.

MIX
Papier aus verantwortungsvollen Quellen
Paper from responsible sources
FSC® C105338

If you have any concerns about our products,
you can contact us on
ProductSafety@springernature.com

In case Publisher is established outside the EU,
the EU authorized representative is:
Springer Nature Customer Service Center GmbH
Europaplatz 3, 69115 Heidelberg, Germany

Printed by Libri Plureos GmbH
in Hamburg, Germany